WHEN GOD WAS
AN ATHEIST
SAILOR

WHEN GOD WAS AN ATHEIST SAILOR

Memories of a Childhood at Sea, 1902–1910

Burgess Cogill

W · W · NORTON & COMPANY

NEW YORK · LONDON

Photograph on p. 79 courtesy of the Peabody Museum of Salem. Photographs on pp. 90, 154, 156, and 164 courtesy of the Muhlman Collection, San Francisco Maritime National Historical Park. All other photographs courtesy of the San Francisco Maritime National Historical Park. Photograph on p. 141 courtesy of the Olmstead Collection, San Francisco Maritime National Historical Park.

The text of this book is composed in 11/14 Monticello, with
display type set in Stymie Extra Bold. Composition and
manufacturing by The Maple-Vail Book Manufacturing Group.
Book design by B. Klein.

First Edition

Library of Congress Cataloging-in-Publication Data
Cogill, Burgess.
When God Was an Atheist Sailor: memories of a childhood at sea /
Burgess Cogill.—1st ed.
p. cm.
1. Cogill, Burgess—Journeys. 2. Snow & Burgess (Schooner)
3. Seafaring life. I. Title.
G540.C6652 1990
910.4′5—dc19 89–3033

ISBN 0-393-02716-3

W. W. Norton & Company, Inc.
500 Fifth Avenue, New York, N. Y. 10110
W. W. Norton & Company Ltd.
37 Great Russell Street, London WC1B 3NU
1 2 3 4 5 6 7 8 9 0

To the memory of my father,
with love and gratitude.

APPRECIATION

My thanks and my appreciation to Bette Bratlien of the National Park Service, David Hull of the J. Porter Shaw Library, Kathryn Slinker of Support Services for Elders, Jane Scribner, and Jo Wheeler, for their help and encouragement in preparing this book for publication. I also wish to thank Lester Anderson for his excellent rendering of the deck plans of *Snow & Burgess* done from my memories.

Some of the photographs in this book are my donation to the National Maritime Museum and are hereby reproduced through their courtesy.

I am happy to leave these memories of my childhood for my daughter, Dagmar Mashbir, and for my grandchildren, Katherine and Eric Mashbir, and for my sister Dagmar's children, Ted and Anne Maxwell.

CONTENTS

Schr. Snow & Burgess
H.H.Morrison

SNOW & BURGESS AS A FIVE-MASTED SCHOONER ... This is how *Snow & Burgess* looked during the first eight years of my young life. Converted from a three-masted ship to a five-masted schooner in 1901, her first trip with my Father as master was the occasion of my birth on September 5, 1902, in the mid-Pacific, miles from land and doctor. It had been agreed if they had a son he would name the boy "Burgess" after the schooner. But as my Father looked down at me, he said very seriously. "If we have a dozen children, there'll never be another one like Burgess." Thus I was born "at large" and named for the proud ship you see.

DEEP SEA NURSERY

Ships and sails and sea
and sounds of moving on forever after;
a playhouse in a hempen coil
instead of tree or garden corner.

Shoes in many foreign ports,
foreign shoes familiar.
Exotics, the everyday sealing wax,
cabbages, the exotics.

Ulysses was king, was god
and god was an atheist sailor;
the telemachae went to school too late
to transfer to another scepter.

Burgess Cogill

PROLOGUE
(10°N-117°W)

SEPTEMBER 5, 1902 dawned as other September days
had dawned in tropical mid-Pacific for countless eons—
hot, sticky, and breathless. There was no breeze to move
the five-masted schooner out of the doldrums, northward to Port Townsend and away from this blue, oil-
smooth expanse of ocean reaching the horizon in all
directions.

The dark-haired young man stood at the after rail
and watched the horizon for the signs of relief that would
first show there. He glanced at the big sails hanging
limp, knowing they would catch the slightest stir of
breeze, and noted grimly that today would be as yesterday—hot, still, windless. For many days now, the
wheel had been lashed and unattended, the logline
hauled in to prevent fouling with the motionless rudder.

This trip had begun a year before—his first trip as
master of the *Snow & Burgess,* newly converted at
Boole's shipyard in Oakland from a three-masted square-
rigger to a five-masted schooner. It had also been his

honeymoon to South Africa, and now below, in the stuffy cabin and beginning her second day, his young wife, Marie was in labor with their firstborn. Here in a spot in mid-Pacific, miles from land and doctor, his child was about to be born.

He continued to gaze at the oil-smooth seascape about him. Many things had happened in the fewer than twenty years he had been in America. He thought back to his confirmation in Denmark at the age of 14 and his apprenticeship on the Danish training ship which began immediately after. A trip around the world began—a trip of discipline and study and work, and when they arrived in Australia he jumped ship, found a job as cabin boy on an American vessel, and thus began his dream. By 1894, at the age of 25, he had attained his naturalization and his master's certificate. By 1901, when he and Mother were married, there had been other ships to his experience, and now it was the big five-masted schooner, *Snow & Burgess,* one of the biggest and fastest ships on the Pacific coast.

It had been a year since the ship had left San Francisco. He had been a whole year married and now his child was coming—all in September. His little Marie had twice rounded Cape Horn, scene of fabled horror and storms, and home of the dread Flying Dutchman who haunted its treacherous seas. Any ship that sighted him, so the story goes, was never heard of again. Africa had given his Marie things to talk of with wonderment for the rest of her life: a tangled tale of Boers and Kafirs and ostrich races at 40 miles an hour; feather boas and plumes; Capetown, Port Elizabeth, and Pretoria and

Johannesburg and Natal (now Durban); the Transvaal and Ladysmith; Jan Christian Smuts; the gold Paul Kruger sovereign she wore as a pin in after years and which spun on a pivotal anchorage; the diamond pin from the Kimberly mines, set in a golden sunburst; and the beginning of her souvenir spoon collection that was to grow impressively as her husband traveled.

They had known when they reached South Africa with their cargo of wheat for the Boer War that a child was coming; had roughly calculated the time in months and the probable location of the birth, at sea, and reached a solution. They would get a nurse from the now-ended Boer War who would go home to England, the long way, to act as midwife when needed. She would experience a sea trip as she might never again chance to encounter, once back in London; she would round the Horn, traverse the expanse of south and north Pacific to the Puget Sound, and once there go by train across Canada, then probably by a steamer to Plymouth, England, and home to London.

He went below, noted for the hundredth time Miss Weston's vigilance and competence and was reassured, but he wished it were over.

Morning dragged on toward noon. He moved toward his chart room, not for the first time that morning. He went directly to one of the cabinets in the small room and removed two large gold coins. Today might be the day; anyway, there was no harm in helping things along. He lifted from its case one of his sextants and went on deck again. Observing that no one was about to see him, he flung one coin over the side for his lovely, spunky little Marie. Then he flung the second into the smooth waters below him—for fair wind!

At the rail, where he stood clear of the mast rigging, he raised his sextant, took a sun shot, then went below to the chart room, unrolled the chart across the big table, and with a small dot marked it—10°N, 117°W. Even though there wasn't a breath of air, ocean currents could carry the vessel beyond yesterday's shooting of the sun, and today's marking could be the birth place of his first-born.

Eight bells struck, then the noon dinner bell. Although he had no appetite, he moved toward the dining room to take his usual place. It was to be another couple of hours before he held his baby in his arms. It had been agreed that if they had a son he would name the boy "Burgess" after the schooner; if the child was a girl, her mother would choose the name. The mother hadn't decided: "Thelma," from one of Hall Caine's novels; or "Lucille," after a long narrative poem of the day.

The time arrived. The baby was born, quickly and without complications—a baby girl. Covered with prickly heat, she was placed in her father's arms; he looked down at the small, red, very wrinkled, ugly infant and said very seriously to his wife, "If we have a dozen children, there'll never be another one like Burgess."

Then with the infant still in his arms, he sent word throughout the ship: "All hands report aft." When they came he shared his wonder—and a water-glass half full of whiskey each, all from the same glass, which doubtless made the wonder even more wonderful.

A year and 24 days later—also in September—when Sister was born, it was in a flat on Buchanan Street in San Francisco, which later burned in the fire of 1906, along with her birth certificate. This time Mother did it properly: a doctor, A. Myles Taylor, and a nurse in attendance. My sister was named Dagmar by Father because every royal household had a Dagmar in the family. I don't think Mother even minded much being preempted on either name. And I don't think Father minded not having a son. He'd already used his son's name for his first daughter.

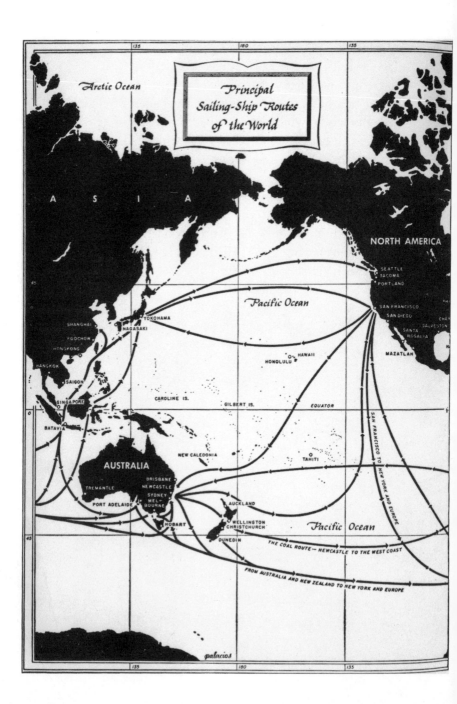

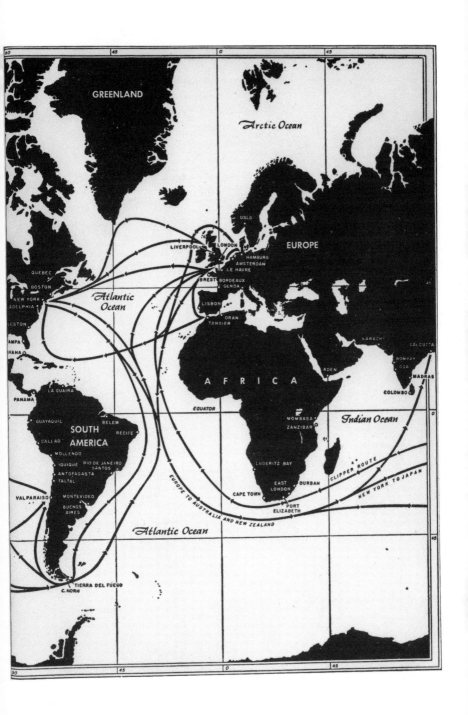

WHEN GOD WAS
AN ATHEIST
SAILOR

A *Life on the Ocean Wave,*
a Home on the Rolling Deep. . . .

Old American Sea Song
Henry Russell (ca. 1838)

THE first eight years of my young life were lived on the *Snow & Burgess*. Of that time, more than half was on the high seas, away from land, away from people except the small community of the ship, whose crew was a total of fourteen men, not counting Mother and Sister and me—sometimes it was even less, depending on the time of year and what weather might be expected. It's not surprising, therefore, that my whole life is colored with memories of the salt, moist smell and feel of the sea, the breezes that carried us on our way, sometimes mild, sometimes wild, the white-laced foam of blue water in open sea, the constantly changing color of sea and sky. Even as a small child, I watched endlessly from the rail the eternal churning, foaming trough of white that followed the ship. We watched it partly because Father watched it but mostly I think because of the scene's own fascination. Skies of brilliant blue met the horizon of deep sapphire seas; leaden skies hung over lead-gray whitecapped waters; days that graduated endlessly between the blue and the gray; black nights without stars and a black sea merging into skies without horizon. Only the sound of the sea, the gentle roll of the ship; only the port and starboard lights somewhere ahead and the sudden flare of the lighted match in the cupped hand of a lookout, smoking on the fo'c's'le head; and from below, the lights from the cabin shining through the skylight. On quieter nights we could see the wake of the ship and the logline glass ticking off the knots of ocean travel.

Gooneys—gray, black, brown, white—flying overhead, or bouncing, bobbing comfortably on the waves below, following the ship and watching for food thrown over the lee side by the cook, Shimoda. One day Father produced a diamond-shaped plate of brass and had the interior cut out so that the diamond was about one-half inch wide all around. Then he wrapped this diamond with strips of salt pork, tied tightly with twine. He attached it to a line and threw it overboard where the gooneys were swimming and floating. When a big brown bird ducked his head into the center of the diamond, Father promptly pulled it up over the side of the ship and easily got the head out of the brass diamond. And then, for all its graceful maneuverability on sea, the gooney was without its sea legs on the gently rolling deck. It spread its huge wings to balance its staggering web-footed gait and very soon gave up its last meal over the clean poop deck! That settled it. Father lifted the large body and sent it over the taffrail. No sooner off the deck from which it could not take off by itself in its seemingly drunken state, the gooney was flying gracefully again to settle on the waves and search for food to replenish the meal left on deck. A man was immediately dispatched from the fo'c's'le, of course, to clean up the mess.

When we were older, and the weather was good, we were allowed to go forward and up on the fo'c's'le head to lean over the bulkhead and watch the spray of the ship as it cut through the water and listen to the rhythm of the ship from the high perch in the prow. We spent hours playing on deck while the men at the wheel changed watches every two hours, calling out the course, 'Nor' by Nor'east," "Sou' by Sou'east," "Aye, aye, Sir" to the mates or captain, and everybody said things like skys'l, mains'l, tops'l. We knew what tacking ship meant, and reefing sails, what a "b'la'ne" pin* was, and the jib boom and bowsprit, and keeping the ship close to the wind, what a chronometer was and what a compass was for. Sometimes I'd take the wheel alongside an A.B.† but not for long. It couldn't last long, especially when you pulled and the seaman just shook his head and pointed to the compass. But just holding it in a straight line without turning wasn't much fun. My frustrated steering days were somewhat compensated for many years later when my small grandson discovered the wheel on the ferryboat *Eureka,* which is tied to the dock at the Maritime Museum's Hyde Street Pier in San Francisco. Hard-a-port, hard to starboard, I remembered to say for him as he pulled the wheel back and forth. When we got home worn

* Belaying pin (pronounced blane pin): a length of iron rail to which ropes are fastened.
† able-bodied seaman.

CHRISTMAS AT SEA ... With a Christmas bow in my hair, I had the place of honor between Father's knees. Dagmar wouldn't hold still in front of Mother, so she is a bit of a blur. We knew that Santa Claus always managed to find us, no matter what part of the ocean we were on, and he would leave dolls and toys and a Christmas tree with ornaments. Our tree is to the right of the big mast that was placed right in the middle of the cabin when they converted *Snow & Burgess* from a three-masted square-rigger to a five-masted schooner. That anyone could do such a thing to an otherwise large and lovely room was quite beyond my Mother's understanding.

out, his mother would ask: "Where did you go today?" "Oh, we covered the waterfront," I'd answer. "What, again!" Oh, yes, and again and again we covered it.

Sometimes we watched for ships although *Snow & Burgess* was usually alone on the vast expanse of sea.

Father's "eagle eye" could pick them out on the far horizon and sometimes he would hold us up on the rail and point for minutes before we found them—tiny ships so far away and an occasional steamer with smoke trailing from her stacks. We watched them all until they dropped over the horizon, wishing they could come closer and Father could hail them and send up signal flags in greeting. His binoculars were always on hand, but sometimes he was familiar enough with the outline to make a guess as to the ship's identity and nationality. When we were close enough, he dipped our own American flag, newly run up, in greeting. Big excitement when ships appeared and came fairly close to us and Father called into the cabin, Ship off the port or starboard bow, or stern—then the flags went up and everyone came up to watch.

On a quiet day at sea, a day of easy sailing and gentle winds, with no other ships around in any direction, Father would get out his code pennants and run them up on a halyard from the poop deck. They had to be aired occasionally, of course, because they might get spotted or mildewed, and Father was great for airing things. In the companionway, he had small varnished cubby holes of mahogany, that snuggly held the pennants, neatly folded and tied and labeled to be found on the instant, and when he decided to air his code flags there was great excitement for us kids. Seeing the million shapes and colors, vertical and horizontal, was almost as good as Fourth of July fireworks at sea. Father was the only one to lay hands on the flags as well as the fireworks. I'm sure he enjoyed this duty. But it

was one of the few times Mother would have a conniption fit, which didn't stop Father, of course. He kept
one eye "peeled," as he put it, on the sea around us to
the limits of the horizon, for it was against marine law
to run up the multicolored, many-shaped international
signals in willy-nilly confusion. Each pennant has a
specific meaning and message which all seafarers
understood and recognized, with a code book. If there
was any confusion as to meaning, the answer was in
the code; it was that specific for seamen the world over,
for every windjammer's needs.

Father was safe and he knew it. There were as yet
no fast steamers to come upon you suddenly, only sailing vessels which depended on the same winds you
did and slow steamers which plodded their way no
faster than *Snow & Burgess* and could be seen by the
trail of black smoke they left against the sky, visible
before the steamer ever was. Those were still the days
of long trips by sail without radio communication when
the only means of guidance was the compass, sextant,
and logline, and charts and the sun and stars and winds
to go by, to give progress in distances, direction, and
days. Steamers were tramps to us and Father held them
in great contempt. The *Matson* and *Dollar* steamers
were few among all the "sails" and really didn't count
much or only in passing.

Looking back, I wonder at the loneliness, the isolation, particularly of longer trips. We were aware—
consciously or unconsciously—of the constant threat
of the sea at even its most benign, but it was not that

that lay behind our fascination with ships that passed within our periphery. I suppose it was the loneliness and isolation.

Father always scoffed, of course, when Mother mentioned possible dangers, but he was up and about at all hours of the day and night, his watch or not, for a surprise prowl in any weather to any part of the ship. Father never smoked when the men could see him, never allowed smoking on deck on watch, except on the fo'c's'le head. But he did allow smoking off watch. I'm sure one reason for the prowl was his unstated fear of fire. When a man fell asleep at the wheel and got off course a point or two he was up on deck in an instant. Anything like wind or sea changes, any increases, slackening off, or veering from course, any break in the normal, steady rhythm of creaks and groans of the ship's sailing patterns would wake him and he was up investigating. He had a separate room and frequently slept with his clothes on day and night. At times of bad weather he'd be in oil skins, wide-brimmed sou-wester strapped under his chin, black rubber boots, appearing at the door of the cabin from time to time, water running off the slick skin of his gear, to reassure Mother and report on progress of the "blow"—that the barometer was lifting, or continuing to fall, that the seas were mountainous and the ship taking on water—or to comment laconically, "One of the worst storms I can remember, as bad as anything off Cape Hatteras," which I knew was bad even before I knew where Cape Hatteras was. Sometimes it was the good

WITH A FAIR WIND, *SNOW & BURGESS* SET NEW RECORDS . . . When we were older, and the weather was good, we were allowed to go forward and up on the fo'c'sle head to lean over the bulk rail and watch the spray of the ship as it cut through the water. We could listen to the rhythm of the ship from our high perch on her prow.

news that the worst of the storm was dropping off and things would be settling down in a few hours, or a maybe a day.

As children, we understood that storms were part of the day or season of the year. The cabin was always snug and warm, and the cabin boy kept the woodbox filled and the fire in the belly of the Franklin stove stoked and glowing and warm. All very reassuring to the snugly imprisoned small fry in the cabin even if the storm somewhat inconvenienced us because of curtailed activity. But we knew Father had everything under control at all times and there was nothing to worry about. In a short time, meals at the table would be resumed, no doubt with a wooden rack on the table for awhile to keep the food and dishes from sliding off. But for the storms of really good blow, meals of one dish in tightly covered tin pails would have to be run from the galley by the dripping cabin boy through decks awash in order to reach their destination. Shimoda, bless him, always managed something like thick pea soup or baked beans and bread for all hands in the clean, shiny, covered lard pails brought out for such times when dishes were of no earthly use.

No one seemed to mind. One time we spent out a storm in bed with meals there, too, and a board fencing us into the bunk to keep us from falling out of bed. A time or two, Sister and I had our meals in bed and stayed there cutting paper dolls and coloring picture books. Mother was on her feet, but just, and we girls were helped out one at a time, as necessary. At times like this the driving wind would plough the ship into a watery mountain ridge that spilled over the fo'c's'le head, and the ship shook with the fury of the seas as the jib boom plunged straight into another water mountain that washed over the ship that shuddered again and again as the storm shrieked and wailed. No need to see it—we could feel its fury. Two men at the wheel in times like this, all hands "on deck" until the gale was over, men scrambling up rigging to take in tops'ls and hanging on for dear life to the booms and foot ropes with the wind and rain beating over them. And always the sounds of running feet on deck above us.

When the storm had settled to regular watches again,

the men who went below came into the dining room for a stiff shot of whiskey before piling into their bunks for a much-needed sleep. The watch on had to wait out the completion of their watch for their drinks. But Father was there, watch on, watch off, until the storm was over. After every storm he called us to see the rainbow. Then, with a change of clothes, he lay down and napped, ready on the instant for the first suggestion of a slapping sail or the slightest shift of a boom.

Much later I learned that my father, Captain Sorensen, had the reputation of being a superb navigator. It was shortly after we were settled ashore, when Father was aboard alone, that he set a record. I quote from an undated *Examiner* clipping that I have:

> During one of the frequent strikes, Sorensen found that when he was ready to leave Port Ludlow there was no crew. All hands consisted of the captain, mates and the cook. The wind was blowing good and plenty from the northwest; but this did not daunt the captain, who proceeded to get his vessel out to sea.
>
> The *Snow & Burgess* came down the coast in record time. That the masts did not give way, perhaps, was due to good luck, for sail was never shortened from the time they were set until anchorage at Meiggs Wharf was reached, and there it was found that *Snow & Burgess* had made the trip in the fastest time on record.

He had the reputation, too, for forcing every advantage from the elements. Later, on longer trips, he broke more records with his big ship, so that *Snow & Burgess*'s time at sea became a matter of betting on the floor of the Merchants Exchange on every long trip he made: Australia, South Africa, South America. He never had an accident or jettisoned a stick of lumber or other cargo—coal or wheat.

There was always deep concern for ships overdue or lost at sea, for Father knew all the captains—at least by name and ship—and many were his friends. Overdue ships were a painful and personal concern for Mother, too. She had come from Denmark to be with her favorite brother, Jack, and learned when she got here that he had been lost in a sudden storm at sea while whaling off the coast of Japan.

The ship of Captain Olsen, one of Father's captain friends, burned at sea and Captain Olsen, his wife, and the crew spent thirty days in a lifeboat before they reached San Francisco. Mrs. Olsen was out of her mind by then. My little Victorian mother empathized with her horror to the point of almost losing her own mind. Another captain friend's wife and small daughter were killed when a boom gave way in a storm and crashed through the cabin.

Sometimes in storms at sea the men had accidents—occasional broken arms or legs, cuts or gashes. Marlin spikes—pointed, wicked weapons—were sometimes dropped from mastheads. Father took no chances that an occasional marlin spike may have been dropped by design, so when men were aloft, we stayed clear of the deck space. But there were accidents. No matter, Father was equal to it all. He applied occasional splints after a large shot of whiskey and got a jar of catgut and medical needles from the medicine-liquor cabinet in the bathroom. Tincture of iodine or arnica was poured liberally into the wound, enough to discourage ambitious bugs that most certainly were lurking on needles kept clean and covered; Father's hands, the dining room where surgery was performed—all were scrupulously clean but hardly operating room sterile at any time. Father did the best he could and having learned to stitch a mean sail in his youth, the medical needles and catgut presented no problem for the master of the ship when surgery was necessary.

Pungent memories of tincture of arnica and iodine, the acrid smell of yellow iodoform used for dressings, together with yards of clean white bandages which Father used. These tools plus the knowledge gleaned from all of the hundred pages of anatomy, hygiene, medicine, and surgery (women's and children's diseases included) from *Scammel's Cyclopedia of Valuable Receipts,* without which he wouldn't have sailed, gave him all he needed to know to handle most medical emergencies. *Scammel's* called for morphia or opium which I don't think Father had or used, for he had plenty of ready-made anesthetic on hand in the form of a water glass of the endemic whiskey, the lifesaver. It was all he needed for them to feel no pain. With the cabin boy to hold the kerosene lamp, to give whatever assistance was needed and stand by quietly observing Father's competence, everything was under control. In port we always called the doctor, which wasn't so interesting—no whiskey before or after to guarantee success for the surgery. Father never lost a patient or had a postoperative infection. No doubt this was due in part to the life seamen led in the back alleys of the world and on the ship which built up a good, tough strain of antibodies to stop incipient surgical infections in their tracks. At the sight of the tough sailors, the bugs curled up and died.

Father's medicine cabinet was a source of fascination. A cabinet of shelves that had a place for each bottle to be instantly and clearly seen. It also contained the liquor bottles to be in ready use for treats in port or at sea, including the port wine bottle with enameled buxom lady on the front from which our morning tonic came. Father's buxomed-lady mustache cup was here, too, and Packer's Tar and Pear soaps, and the bars of Castille soap from which slabs were cut. The Pears' soap wrapper still says, "Must be started in childhood for beautiful women!" I ought to add a note about the liquor in the medicine cabinet. Father tolerated no liquor on the ship except under his control. It was understood by everyone: *no liquor* except what he doled out. He was fairly liberal with treats for special occasions, like Christmas, rough weather rewards, and, of course, medicinal use, as he saw it. But if he thought anyone was drinking at sea or had a private stash in spite of orders, he went through the fo'c's'le or even the mates' rooms and pitched it overboard. One of his searches of the fo'c's'le revealed a set of brass knuckles, to Mother's horror when he showed her. I didn't have to be told what they were for, either, when he put them on.

Father was big on fresh air, good food, exercise, and of course a little tonic, like port wine, to put iron in the blood. In the morning at sea, we small girls awoke to the sound of his mixing our tonic in the bathroom across the companionway—beating raw egg yolks and sugar (the whites were thrown out), adding a table-spoon of port, then dividing it into two shot glasses. He put them on a tray and brought them to us in our bunks. Sometimes we were awake and waiting, some-times asleep, but whichever it was, "Time to get up and dress for breakfast." But first our tonic, and he waited for us to finish, which didn't take long. Even our pet cats came running when they heard Dad mix-ing or heard the squeak of the cork in the neck of the port bottle. They got the spoon and the bowl to lick when Father was through mixing and it always amused him that they purred their heads off over the last of the tonic.

Breakfast at seven (6 bells), dinner at noon (8 bells), supper at five (2 bells)—the sea schedule was set, invi-olate. Watches of four hours on, four off, beginning with 8 bells each around the clock. The man at the wheel changed at the stroke of the bell, first struck on the after deck, immediately echoed by the man on watch on the fo'c's'le head. The full complement for *Snow &* *Burgess* constituted eight able-bodied seamen and cook, cabin boy, carpenter, first and second mates, and cap-tain. The crew was split for each watch—four seamen with captain and second mate, four with first mate. The first mate had meals with the captain and family, the second mate with the carpenter, unless we were in port, when there was only one table.

As mentioned earlier, Father kept irregular hours and watches at sea, not only in storms. He had an

REAPER, ALL SAILS SET . . . A classic view of the three-masted down-easter, built in Bath, Maine in 1876. Captain A. P. Lorentzen of San Francisco bought her in 1876. My father was her master before he took over *Snow & Burgess* in 1901. The damaged glass negative has suffered the fate of many such fine plates, but the majestic spread of her sails is still intact in this view.

unpleasant habit—for seamen not doing their jobs—of quietly materializing anywhere, anytime. And when we were awake, we were very familiar with this pattern. A man at the wheel at night found it pretty uncomfortable to be caught asleep, even for a minute. Usually a quiet, laconic man with orders given softly and just once, there were times when he roared and the effect was electrifying. It was probably well-known, too, that he could use his fists like a champion when it was necessary, that he kept in trim by morning sessions with a punching bag fastened to the ceiling of the bedroom, and removed when not in use.

The rhythmic clip-clip-clip of the leather bag against the ceiling is another familiar sound of my childhood that I could recognize anywhere. Like the regular groans of the ship cutting through seas and the rhythmic creaks of the masts to the pressure of wind on sails. And smells of manila rope, and tar and oakum caulking of deck planks, and for the rest of my life the smell of coffee roasting on a clear, windy day in San Francisco—somewhere around Third and Berry Streets there must have been and still may be a coffee plant; the cook, too, always roasted all our coffee. Wherever I am when any of these sounds or smells reach me, I'm instantly transported back to the ship and my childhood.

Fair weather at sea was always something to bask in, especially when we were without deckload. The full length of the decks from the fo'c's'le head, including the galley and carpenter shop, up to the poop deck were ours to roam and to explore. Coils of rope along the way were ours to play house in, or just to snuggle into in the warmth of the main deck, sheltered beneath the bulwarks. We played house in the coiled ropes for hours with ladies and furniture cut from magazines. When we tired of that, loving our cats and dogs in the sunshine was pleasant for both of us, and the cats and dogs, too. Neither species was allowed in the cabin with the carpets and velvet seat covers, but the animals got loved sufficiently in spite of this deprivation. We had only female cats and dogs, no males to embarrass Father and Mother with difficult questions.

We knew, of course, that babies were brought by storks over large expanses of sea and that Santa Claus came with his reindeer and left Christmas trees and ornaments and dolls and toys no matter what part of the ocean we were on. Somebody brought you a puppy or kitten from ashore but once something strange happened to my brown dog, Mary Jane. I saw her in a corner of the cabin and puppies were coming out of her. In the excitement of the discovery, I called for Mother and Father. They came right away. Mother whisked me away (although she had been brought up on a farm in Denmark) and left Father to cope with Mary Jane's predicament. The next day when I saw Mary Jane again, there were no puppies about, nor the next day, or the next. After that I didn't bother to look and I didn't ask Mother or Father. Somehow I knew they weren't the proper source for asking and there wasn't anyone else. Information was freely given about matters we were expected to know, but otherwise questions weren't encouraged. Many years later— almost three-quarters of a century later, in fact—in talking to my grandchildren about life in the far-back history of other days, and customs and life at the turn of the century, I've tried to make clear to them some of the differences: children should be seen and not heard, "bad" words got your mouth washed out with soap, you never talked back to or disputed your parents or

Rolph, an Ill-Fated Barkentine . . . Bad luck dogged the *Rolph*. She was rammed in the fog on the Thames in 1919. And in 1921, her voyage became the setting for a sensational series of charges of cruelty against the first mate, Frederic Hansen. Father had hired him in Australia and paid him off in Chile. The newspapers had a field day with the story of a "hell ship," and Father was to stand trial for his responsibility in the affair. This never happened, as Hansen was captured and imprisoned for five years—his second offense, the first had been murder.

any other adult. Beautiful, 10-year-old grandchild Katie challenged me immediately, indignantly, reasonably: "Suppose you *had* insisted on knowing, suppose you *had* talked back, what would possibly have happened, Grandmother?"

I thought and thought while Katie watched, awaiting my answer. Finally, I said, "I guess the sky would have fallen all over my head."

"Grandmother, be sensible," said Katie in her severest, firmest tones. *"What would have happened?"*

All that came to me after the falling sky was the classic line, with finger pointed, from *East Lynne* or some such melodrama, "Go, and never darken my door again," or the words from the old song, "The picture that was turned towards the wall." Both these reactions were current and commonplace in my childhood, and frightening in their dire threat. I took the whole subject up with contemporaries, male and female, many years later in a rather lively discussion. What *would* have happened? We all understood the original premise too well; we'd all been brought up the same way, but going back in time and feeling to those days, we couldn't make any sense of it. I guess this was just the way things were then, so Katie never got a sensible answer.

A day of gentle trades was always good for repairs and painting and mending and clean-up. Other kinds of days weren't good, and neither was time in port. While in port, the ship was loading and unloading and the subsequent confusion didn't allow space, in any case. Anyone who wasn't part of the confusion kept out of the way of swaying booms and hardwood and iron tackles and blocks and sudden uncoiling ropes, snapping skyward in a flash. At sea, there were over-the-bulwarks deck-loads of lumber or logs secured by heavy chains, so obviously no work could be done, and only the vitally necessary crew could navigate the windy, unsheltered top of the cargo load. In a stiff breeze, a minimum of traffic was in order. But when the ship

THE WRECK OF THE *ROSE MAHONY* ... After a life-long career as master of sailing ships with no accidents on his record, a freak hurricane off Florida lifted all 2051 tons of *Rose Mahony* out of the water and left her stranded, to be sold for scrap. Irony upon irony, her insurance had expired midway in her Panama Canal crossing and was not renewed because the big five-masted schooner was so close to her destination.

came into San Francisco from sea, weather and cargo permitting, the masts were scraped and oiled by men in bosun's chairs, new white paint glistened wherever white paint belonged, iron work was chipped and red-leaded, decks caulked and holy-stoned.

We might be viewing stereopticon slides in the cabin, fascinated with the change from one- to three-dimensional views, or playing with our big dolls with real hair and clothes that came off (which was never done on deck!) when Father would appear in the door of the cabin and call out in his loud sailor voice, "Get into your gear, fellas. All hands on deck." We dropped the dolls, got rid of their lace dresses, and were instantly ready for the legitimate defacement that this was sure to mean. Excitedly, we got into rubber boots and got our brooms for washing down decks, while the sailors hauled water in canvas buckets from over the side and sloshed the decks and scrubbed, too. Or Carpie (the nickname for the carpenter) was pumping out the bilges, which we sometimes made use of for the same purpose. Bilge water was the clean salt sea water that had seeped into the ship. When the main deck was fresh and clean with salt water which had run off the lee scuppers, everyone left, the same ones to await the next call to wash down decks. Getting in and scrubbing right along with the men was lovely, serious business. Normally, we had to be very careful not to dirty anything on deck. We could play in the coils of rope, but we couldn't untwist them. And we could spill nothing. But in washing down decks, anything went—it was the most fun thing we could do. And Father always let us do it. If we got wet, it didn't matter. Mother was sitting there, she could change us and she didn't say anything.

Chipping rust, like painting the white woodwork around the ship, was especially exciting. This was done less often than washing down decks but was a bigger and longer operation. For the chipping, Father got light chisels and small hammers for us, and all the iron works about the ship—hatch coamings, pin rails on masts, bitts—were chipped as we saw the sailors chip them. When everything was clean (not necessarily our doing), the red lead went on. We got some small brushes and a small can one-third full of red lead or white paint, clean rags, and the caution: Try not to spill the paint but if you do, wipe it up immediately. Then he was off and we'd go to it. We'd work on the clean iron on the inside of the bulwarks, which were painted white, as I remember, from the stringers to the pin rail. The only pictures I have showing this section do not show white paint here. This may have been a later decision of Father's but I distinctly remember painting designs of great beauty, and about the time I'd lean over to admire them, a sailor would come along and cover the whole thing solid white. I learned to move far enough ahead of him to at least finish and admire my designs, if not save them for posterity. And Father, of course, was never around to appeal to. All over the ship at any one time, he would be missing for these moments of delicate judgment.

Apparently Father's credo of child-rearing was similar to the preacher's (or almost!), "To everything there is a season and a time to every purpose under the Heaven," except disciplining his two small girls. If he couldn't handle the situation by just a slight constrained disapproval, he disappeared and left the field to some handy lesser surrogate authority.

Things to do at sea were endless: for example, there was the galley with its flour bins and water. If you were very quiet and didn't waken Shimoda from his afternoon nap, you could get quite far along with your baking. And all the great tools in the carpenter's shop! In no time at all you could make a small doll table with dowels and assorted pieces of wood stacked neatly in bins for Carpie's instant use, or get warmed at the fire from the donkey engine which was always burning to some degree. Getting steam up took time and one never knew when the donkey engine would be needed. Or just making curls with Carpie's planes and small pieces of 2×4's and hanging them in our straight hair. The carpenter shop was a really lovely place to play because, like the galley, it was always so neat, and Carpie was a patient man, not volatile like Shimoda, who held his head in his hands and hollered, "Jesus Christ, Jesus Christ, my galley, my galley," along with some Japanese we didn't understand.

Carpie (or "Chips," but really Carl) was good-natured and easygoing, a mild man of huge muscles and rolling gait. He was the only person I ever saw as a child with muscles that gleamed and rippled as he worked. With blond curly hair and blue eyes, Carpie was the Swedish version of Longfellow's village smithy and every bit as fascinating. We spent a lot of time with him, and I always think of him wiping his hands on wads of cotton waste, wiping the engine and tools and benches.

Many a sunny day was spent in airing spare and used sails stored in the lazaret, checking them for rips or worn spots in the sewing, replacing the worn spots with new canvas so that an otherwise unusable sail would be like new again. Airing the fresh new sails kept them from rotting in storage. An A.B. and Father would carefully go over all the sails. Then the sailor

CAPTAIN SORENSEN (CENTER) AND CREW . . . Born in Denmark in 1869, as Anton Holmgaard Sorensen, Father got his master's certificate and his naturalization papers at the age of 25. By the time he was 31 he was Captain of *Snow & Burgess*. At the turn of the century, Pacific Coast sailors were known as "The Scandinavian Navy," made up of immigrant Finns, Swedes, and Danes, with a sprinkling of Germans. Like our Shimoda, the cooks were apt to be Japanese or Chinese.

would set to work on the main deck, huge sails spread around him. We watched the leisurely movements as he cut the canvas to measure and threaded the four-inch long, three-sided heavy sail needle with twine that had been heavily waxed with yellow chunks of wax ridged deeply by previous use. Then he would adjust the leather strap affixed to a knobby brass palm "thimble" and go to work on the sails in neat, even stitches. Each stitch required the forced push of the brass "thimble" against the palm of the hand to get the needle through the layers of canvas.

We never attempted to sew sails, just watched and tried on the big "palms," and examined the needles and wax and balls of twine. One look at the canvas was enough to tell us we'd never make the push but we spent hours watching the sailor doing it, then watching him smoothing out the heavy seam with his big bare hands. Father had put in his own time before the mast mending sails and could, on occasion, show his ability with a sea shirt button—heavy thread, button, big needle. Another of my early recollections is Mother's mirth when she saw one of his sewing jobs. But Father kept his ditty box supplied, like all proper sailors, with the wherewithall to self-sufficiently handle any emergency, and a loose button could be an emergency. Sometimes Mother cut through the yards of thick thread that would have held a button past the disintegration of the entire shirt, and removed the button. But Father never asked her to do it. Sewing on buttons was sailors' work, as was patching sea pants or shirt.

When a patch no longer sufficed, there was always the slop chest. The large varnish-covered box—about seven-feet by three-feet wide and three-feet deep, all neatly stocked with clothing the men might require—stretched across one end of the large bedroom. The slop chest was not used too much on shorter trips but was vitally necessary on longer trips. Men shipped on with a minimum of clothes after a layoff ashore, sometimes with little more than what they had on. Withdrawals from the slop chest were charged against the pay coming when they signed off. For longer trips the chest was fuller and generally more complete with a greater assortment of sizes of socks, long underwear, workshirts, towels, salt water soap, and whatever else was needed like blankets, coats, and shoes. Father selected whatever was asked for and brought it to the dining room.

There was no bath or shower in the fo'c's'le, only the toilet—which I never saw even when the ship was without crew. The fo'c's'le itself was stale and windowless. Air came from two doors, which were generally open except in storms. One was on the port side, the other the starboard, both under the shelter of the fo'c's'le head. Four bunks lined each side. Many times in the galley I saw the slide-door near the stove open and meals for the crew passed into the fo'c's'le. I do not remember seeing, since I was never inside, any stove for heating the room. Perhaps heat from the galley where the stove was always going was enough.

How the men before the mast bathed or washed or laundered their clothes remained a mystery until the South American trip when I saw them, two at a time, haul water from over the side and slosh it over each other and wash clothes on the lee side in pails of salt water with salt water soap.

By that time I'd been introduced to salt water baths and didn't like them one bit. Hair was the worst, sticky with salt, but the ship's supply of fresh water had to be conserved for drinking and cooking. You could get used to it, as we did. I still remember the first screaming time: children were seen *and* heard but Mother was equal to it. One yank and a shake! You had to be washed and bathed and, worst of all, hair washed and that was all there was to it!

For washing their clothes, the sailors sometimes used expedient shortcuts. They tied a rope around their clothes, lowered them over the lee side to beat and thrash in the water against the ship as we sailed. This was the only time I saw clothes drying on the deck. They strung a rope also on the lee side below the bulwarks and in this way they dried without being seen, flying over the side of the ship. Permission probably was granted for this unseemly irregularity, but Mother, who loved the sun and the wind on her clean clothes, should have been so lucky.

Washing and ironing our clothes was one of the few household tasks of Mother's while we were on the ship. But in all my young life at sea, I never saw our clothes being dried; it was as though the time between washing and ironing didn't exist. Mother washed in the bathroom, in two large galvanized tubs set up in the bathtub. They were filled by the cabin boy, Bob, with steaming water run from the galley. Bob also ran the hot water for our weekly baths from the galley. The laundry finished, it disappeared with the help of Bob, probably into the lazaret (pronounced "lazareet"), and was not seen until with Bob's help it went to the galley in a large basket for ironing, where Mother could heat her irons along with the breakfast meal on the big, black, railed, wood-burning range while Shimoda slept. When we were in port, bedding and Father's white starched shirts and collars went to the laundry. Mostly Shimoda and Mother visited and talked about Japan, his family, and when his next visit would be; he and Mother got along very well. She learned to make kidney sautée from Shimoda; he learned pumpernickel bread from Mother, which he made occasionally for us as a special treat.

Mother made all our clothes at sea on a treadle sewing machine backed into a closet when not in use. She even helped Santa sometimes with doll clothes. Our play clothes for sea were high-necked, long-sleeved, dark, printed calico dresses and black bloomers worn with high-laced black shoes and long black stockings. The dark stuff so it wouldn't "show the dirt." I've wondered since about those long black stockings that ran up under our voluminous black bloomers—however were they held up? Memory fails me here again but held up they were with no bare thigh showing, no matter what the activity or temperature. Our dress-up clothes were ruffled dimity with lace insertions, and ruffled dotted-Swiss and China silk. We wore many sheer ruffled petticoats. All these were worn with button shoes of black patent leather and white kid-tops, all with a dab of Mother's Florida water. This uniformity of dress lasted well into grammar school before enough joint rebellion could be mustered against the sameness of our dress to allow for the individuality of separate tastes to develop. All the sewing was done at sea because in port, what with entertaining and being entertained, there was just no time.

Bob cleaned the cabin. He scattered damp newspaper over the carpet to catch the dust as he swept with a straw broom. Then he dusted, washed the mirrors, cleaned the brass strips on the stairs of the companionway that were placed across the treads to prevent slipping. He made Mother's big double bed, Sister's bunk and my bunk, cleaned and made up Father's stateroom. Then he cleaned the brass gimbals that held all the lamps to keep them balanced with the roll of the ship. Kerosene lamps had to be refilled, the smoke cleaned from the glass shades, the wicks trimmed. All the lamps in the cabin had to be done, in the dining room and pantry, in the two mates' rooms, as well as kerosene stoves for our bathroom snack-cooking and the pantry heating stoves, particularly necessary for the essential all-night strong coffee.

Polishing the brass in the cabin, shining the cuspidors and reading lamps was fascinating to us, although this was another ship job we only watched. Bob went to work with rags and a can of Bennett's Brilliant Shine Metal Polish; the dark red label, attesting to "brilliant and lasting luster with least labor" had a picture of Mr. Bennett on the front, small beard, large moustache, impeccable in black suit, white shirt with stiff wing collar—the whole topped off by the white boutonniere. The picture definitely had class on a par with the actresses we found in glossy magazines we pored over. Having looked at his picture on the dark red cans so many times, I remember Mr. Bennett well.

Periodically, the canvas-covered lifeboats on deck had to be checked and the water and hardtack stored in them changed. One boat was on a rack on the main deck, the other was over the stern on davits and guyed to the ship. Fresh water in the lifeboats we weren't interested in but this was the only time we got hard-tack—to Father's and Mother's disgust but to our gusto. We ate them warmed with butter, mostly. We loved the large, hard, thick, unsalted crackers. Probably we were the only ones on the ship who did; we ate our fill and the rest went to Davy Jones's locker to feed the fish. They were always perfectly good but the large, square, airtight cans in the lifeboat couldn't be expected to last forever. It would be awful to depend on this to sustain you if the containers had sprung a leak. Once opened the cans couldn't be closed airtight again.

Food—with no means of refrigeration—was a very important concern at sea. There was a meat locker with heavy butcher storage doors in which were kept sides of beef, barrels of corned beef, ham, salt pork and lard, sides of bacon, dried codfish, smoked tongues, barrels of salmon bellies. In another locker were kept canned foods: fish, seafood, chipped beef, all kinds of canned vegetables and fruits to supplement the fresh food we started out with. There was flour, oatmeal, dried fruits, raisins and nuts, stacks of canned milk, and Eagle Brand condensed milk. Dried onions and potatoes were spread on the locker floor to retard their spoilage.

Snow & Burgess always sailed with a well-stocked food locker and a good cook, Shimoda, who stayed with the ship for years, as did the cabin boy, Bob. In fact, most of the officers, too, stayed with my father for years. He was generous with them, but he expected perfection, too. Shimoda had full sway over menus and

Snow & Burgess as a **Three-Masted Ship** . . . This painting shows *Snow & Burgess* as she looked when she was launched in 1878 from Thomaston, Maine. She was 228.5 feet long by 41.5 feet wide and 24.7 feet in depth, and had a gross tonnage of 1655.49. San Francisco's Captain A. P. Lorentzen bought her in 1900 and a year later she was converted by Boole's shipyard in Oakland to the five-masted schooner.

preparation, as well as submitting the orders to carry them out. Hence, meals for and aft were always good and food plentiful. In addition to the three regular meals a day, at sea there were always night snacks for the crew and cabin. Some of the night meals put out were canned salmon with sliced onions and vinegar, sardines, and cheese and bread. The coffee made Mother shudder. In the first place it got stronger and more syrupy as the dawn came up and Mother's comment whenever the subject was mentioned was a horrified:

"If you put the spoon in the middle of the cup it stands straight up!"

She wouldn't touch it, but Father had his share and drank it without comment with Eagle Brand condensed milk, which must have helped. I never tasted it. During the day, Mother made coffee on the bathroom stove, especially for midafternoon snacks in the cabin which we all had. With the tinned crackers we had anchovies from small barrels, smoked eels and sardines, canned tamales, and in warm weather, beer—a shot glass each for Sister and me. We had jams and Danish cheese, and Limburger was a great favorite on crusty fresh-baked pumpernickel with tinned Danish butter. No wonder the mates, carpenter, cook, and cabin boy stayed on for years. Sailors, on the other hand, changed every trip, but sometimes after a layoff even they returned.

The reference to British ships and seamen as "Lime-juicers" and "Limeys" attests to the awareness of the importance of diet to seamen. I imagine a whole nation of seamen characterized by an unusual aspect of their diet! Nobody seemed to know more than that lime juice prevented scurvy, and all British seamen got their quota of it. In Father's edition of Ainsley's *Examiner In Seamanship* ("Being the Seamanship required of Candidates for Certificates of Competency in the Ordinary and Extra Examinations, arranged in Questions and Answers also, Definitions, Adjustment of the Sextant, Law of Storms, &c* with Plates of the Commercial

*&c-Archaic form of etcetera (etc.).

54

Code of Signals, &c, 43rd Edition, printed in London, Price 2 shillings," but no publishing date) one of the questions is: "Q. When do you commence to serve lime juice and how much to each man? A. On the 11th day after leaving port; one ounce to each man." Father did not need to do this because of the bountiful and varied stores of food that he provided.

I also noted that Ainsley was a teacher of navigation and the author of several books on the subject. Of the 223 pages in the *Examiner In Seamanship,* Ainsley gives all of nine pages, at the very end of the book, to steamers! So much for steam. He probably shared Father's contempt for steamers that any damned fool could navigate, but a big sailing vessel took knowledge and skill of a high order.

At night after supper we walked the dogwatch with Father and Mother and the first mate on the poop deck, back and forth, back and forth. This was almost a ritual. We walked every night unless gales or storms prevented it. We learned on such nights: "Red sky at night, sailor's delight, red in the morning, sailors take warning." We walked some nights coated and capped and scarfed and mittened, and hated it, longing for the snug warmth of the cabin below. To this day, I don't know how Father managed it but we walked—no hassle, no arguments, no revolt (although Mother was close to it at times, especially when she was reading comfortably below). But when Father called we all went. Nobody could go to bed without the salt breezes zinging through your lungs and into your bloodstream and into your cheeks and eyes, especially when we'd been cooped up all day and the cabin was stuffy and hot and airless from shut doors.

In general, though, these walks were very pleasant. We watched the evening dews appear like jewels on the paintwork and rails as we walked; we watched the stars: the North Star, Venus, Big Dipper; fine, full moonlit nights with the sea about us catching its silver in the waves. We walked to blue, blue skies of fullest moon with only the big stars shining; to black velvet star-studded skies with matching sea; to dark blue skies of crowding stars that could almost be reached by our small hands. While we walked, there was the rhythmic lap of the sea against the hull of the sailing ship.

On balmy nights, Father would bring up his accordion and play for us. Father was self-taught and played by ear. He played some of the melodramatic ballads of the day, and he loved waltzes and loved ragtime, but didn't play much of it ("Alexander's Ragtime Band"). Mostly, though, his repertoire consisted of "The Blue Danube," "Over the Waves," "The Merry Widow Waltz," "Sweet Rosy O'Grady," and the song about Casey who waltzed with the strawberry blonde "while the band played on," "Sidewalks of New York," "Take Me Out to the Ballgame," although I don't remember his ever going to a ballgame, "Cuddle Up a Little Closer," and "I Wonder Who's Kissing Her Now." The nights when Father played we got to stay up a bit later, but when he began "Sweet Marie Come to Me" we knew it was bedtime for the kids. Marie was Mother's first name and there wasn't much use to appeal to either Father or Mother after that!

The melodies I remember best were the story-songs that Mother sang to us. "A Passing Policeman" who found a lost little girl, dried her tears for her and kindly offered to find her mother only to discover it was the selfsame wife who had left him (the policeman) when this selfsame little girl was only a baby! "After the Ball" told of many a heart that was aching because of some misunderstanding not thoroughly understood by us, but we were gripped by the pathos of the words, and the music, too. At Mother's knee we learned the Stephen Foster songs and "Come Back to Erin," "The Preacher and the Bear," and "H-A-Double-R-I-G-A-N Spells Harrigan." My introduction to the Civil War was "Just Before the Battle, Mother," "Rally, Round the Flag, Boys," and "The Blue and the Grey," one of whom lay buried at Appomattox. We sang "I Picked a Lemon in the Garden of Love, Where They Say Only Peaches Grow," "The Man Who Broke the Bank at Monte Carlo," "My Wife's Gone to the Country, Hooray, Hooray, I Love My Wife but Oh, You Kid, My Wife's Gone Away," "Ta-Ra-Ra-Boom-De-Ay," "Won't You Come Over to My House, Won't You Come Over and Play," and "I Don't Want to Play in Your Yard, I Don't Like You Anymore, You Can't Holler Down the Rain Barrel or Slide Down the Cellar Door." "My Irene Is the Village Queen; She's the Queen of the Village Green; and When She Plays on the Ay-cordeen, A Sweeter Gal You Never Seen," could make you jiggle all over. "Hello, Central, Give Me Heaven" was a fearsome takeoff on the novelty of the telephone. And who doesn't remember the whodunit: "Who Threw

57

the Overalls in Mrs. Murphy's Chowder?" "She Was Bred (or 'bread,' as we children always thought of it) in Old Kentucky," to which we could add gleefully in song, understanding in full the not-so-subtle double-entendre, "But in Boston She Was Beans."

I can't leave the subject without mention of three very special favorites. "Show me the way to go home, I'm tired and I wanna go to bed. I had a little drink about an hour ago and it went right to my head." And the second: "I'm afraid to go home in the dark. Every-day the papers say there's a robbery in the park, so I sit alone in the YMCA singing just like a lark, Oh, there's no place like ho-ome but I couldn't go home in the dark." Both these songs were sung punctuated with hics at the proper places. The third: "There was I waiting at the Church, left in the lurch, of course, and getting a note saying his wife wouldn't let him meet me." Is anyone having a conniption fit over songs that are popular today?

Some nights the sailors entertained with harmonica solos and songs from the fo'c's'le head which wafted back on the still night air as we walked and listened; sea chanties perhaps, for the music was different from that aft, but I never really heard them sung until the South American trip. Very pleasant to listen to; I've often wondered if they listened to us.

Every day as the sun approached the meridian, Father came on the poop deck, sextant in hand, and moved toward the rail. If I was on deck, I'd move toward him as he waited for the chronometer to reach the appointed time for taking the sun. While he waited he made adjustments of small glass panels on the sextant—green, several shades of red, brown—to shut out the glare and then he held the sextant up for me, directing it, so that I saw a dark ball without glare through a colored frame. At the proper time, he'd "shoot" the sun and read the logline glass, then we'd go below to the chartroom to make the day's entries on the charts. When he was through computing the ship's position and distance from the previous day and drawing a line to indicate the new position on the shart and penciling in the distance in miles, we walked: here's where we are today; today we made a rather longish line on the chart, or a short one, or a tangent line; Why? Because the wind carried us off, or was fair for us or only light, so that we made many or not so many knots. Mother was interested in the knots, but only the larger amounts, like 12, 13, or 14 knots an hour. She always seemed pleased, as was Father, when we made 14 knots by Father's estimate, which was the ship's top speed and very good sailing for a big wooden ship over any one day.

Father and I had big discussions on latitude and longitude and why he had so much figuring to do and had to consult his copy of Davis's *Sun's True Bearing* or *Azimuth Tables 30°N to 30° S* (London, 1900). Its preface describes some of the complications of navigation: "The increasing quantity of iron used in construction of wooden ships and the increasing number of iron ships, render a ready and simple mode of ascertaining the duration of the compass of paramount importance to the safety of the vessel, as well as to insure

Snow & Burgess Was a Grand Sight to See . . . Moving smartly before the wind, she was one of the biggest and fastest ships on the Pacific Coast. My father, Captain Sorensen, had a reputation of being a superb navigator. He had the reputation, too, of forcing every advantage from the elements. He broke so many records that *Snow & Burgess's* time at sea became a matter of betting on the floor of the Merchants Exchange on every long trip he made.

a quick passage by steering exactly the course intended. As is well-known, the deviation is no constant, either with regard to the direction of the ship's head, or her position on the globe, the careful navigator is therefore alive to the necessity of checking his compass by observation, the greater the facility rendered him for this purpose the more frequently will the observations be made."

Sometimes we would stand over the charts and Father would point out 10°N–117°W and have me repeat it, disregarding the fractions of latitude and longitude for the basic essentials, and always with the patience and proper seriousness befitting the importance of that base spot on the bluebooked chart. I would be shown the place of my birth and I wasn't to forget it, ever.

On days of fog and rain and storm when no sun was seen, Father checked the binnacled, gimballed compass before the wheel on deck and the logline glass, and made his calculations by "dead reckoning." In a day or two or three there'd be sun again, and the ship's course could then be corrected to the gnat's eyebrow it usually was set to follow.

Fog at sea was not so unusual, perhaps because like the storms, we were mostly inside and paid little attention to it. Foghorns, pumped by hand from the fo'c's'le head, blowing their eerie, haunting, mournful wail at regular intervals day and night; going on deck to witness the shock and strangeness of cottony mist pressing onto the ship, all around, obliterating the fo'c's'le head and sea that surrounded us at all times, and over all the perpetual wail of the foghorn. Once I remember seeing the hull of a large black steamship pass by us in thick fog, close enough to see the blurred outline that was there, but not close enough to touch us, just slipping by close and away as silently as she appeared. Our red-green port—starboard lights were lit as usual, but she didn't seem to see them. Foghorns all around and she just loomed at our side and as quietly disappeared. Father was fit to be tied for awhile after that one.

Only once we took guests on board for a trip north from San Francisco. We took the wife of the owner, Capt. A. P. Lorentzen, his son and daughter and a young friend of theirs, Allen Boyle, to Seattle for the Potlatch Festival in the summer of 1909.

It was the first time we'd ever met Capt. Lorentzen's second wife and family because there had been a rather upsetting divorce from his first wife, who was Mother's aunt. Then there was a belated marriage to his second wife which had occurred just before she came aboard, and as Lorentzen was *Snow & Burgess*'s owner, the whole situation became very complicated and sticky, at least for Mother. Kathleen (the girl) and Andrew, Jr., were a few years older than Sister and I, and friends for us. The relationship clicked and lasted a whole lifetime, but until the death of Mother's aunt it was walking a tightrope between two families for two small girls. Understandably, we'd been taught not to lie, but also we were taught not to tell Mother's aunt that we'd seen the second family. Whenever she got us alone, she started insidiously questioning us. Mother had already been through it and handled it in an adult fashion, but Sister and I squirmed to her "loving" capture and questions. Needless to say we didn't like seeing her.

The trip north with three young guests (the mothers somehow didn't count) was marvelous. It was summer and the weather was fine. With no deckload,

FRIENDS AT SEA WERE A RARE TREAT . . . Dagmar and I (from left to right) are wearing big sunbonnets and holding our pet dogs. Captain Lorentzen's daughter, Kathleen, sits beside us. In back are Allen Boyle and Andrew Lorentzen, with our cabin boy, Bob Wakamea. Captain A. P. Lorentzen owned *Snow & Burgess* but the only trip we took with them as guests was to the Potlash Festival in Seattle in 1909. It was summer and the weather was fine. With no deckload, we had the run of the ship and the two boys were out of their skulls with excitement and into everything. Once they even locked the cook in the meat locker—but *only once.*

we had the run of the ship. The two boys were out of their skulls with excitement and into everything. They were up and down the rigging most of the time and once locked the cook in the meat locker—but *only once.* Father was in charge of the boys and here he had no trouble at all! He let them run wild, but any interference with the crew, especially the cook, was not to be tolerated again.

We may have gone short-handed for crew that trip—it had been done before for more compelling reasons but that's the only way I can account for enough sleeping arrangements. Possibly we were without a second mate; possibly also a carpenter. But the trip up was lovely, and Bob, our cabin boy, enjoyed the boys who were nearly his own age, even though the whole business gave him extra work, but extra fun, too. I'm sure Father was as protective of him as he could be; Bob was very much a favorite with him.

Once north, we all went to Seattle for the Potlatch Festival of the Alaska-Yukon-Pacific Exposition, and saw the totems from Alaska and all the sparkling fountains of a great fair. It was the beginning of lovely, lifelong friendships. In the same year, 1909, the Portola Festival was celebrated in San Francisco. We went to it with Ted, roaming the night streets of San Francisco with joy in the fun and music and gaiety.

As I Was A-Walking Down Paradise Street
Singing Way-ay, Blow the Man Down . . . .

CAPE FLATTERY and Tatoosh Light, Straits of Juan de Fuca, Father had had his "eagle eye" out, scanning the landscape for some time before he was the first to spot them. Then he'd call down to the cabin, "Tatoosh Light, Cape Flattery" and we knew we were about to make the long sail through the Strait of Juan de Fuca to Puget Sound to wherever we were going—Port Gamble, Port Ludlow, big lumber centers then, their bays filled with the masts of many sailing ships; to beautiful Whidby Island and Ladysmith and New Westminster where turbaned Hindus worked the docks as *Snow & Burgess* loaded or unloaded. They gave us candy, but Mother wouldn't let us eat it because, she said, they were lousy. I was to be lousy too one day, to her everlasting Danish horror, but not from the Hindu longshoremen of New Westminster.

I have the definite feeling now that I always knew when we were near land, that there was a certain feel-

---

* Sea chantey, "Blow the Man Down."

ing about the way the ship handled herself through the water that was different from the sounds and movements she made in deep water. It was a feeling of wanting to say when I was told we were near land, "Yes, I know, I feel it," though I never did say this. When we approached land the sea felt different, was different, the birds were different. Gooneys dropped away, land birds appeared almost as if by magic overnight. The color of the sea changed though there may have been no land in sight yet, at least for small eyes. Sometimes we'd make the Strait late in the day and we'd go to sleep with the tug towing us as darkness fell. In the morning I'd wake knowing we were anchored in the bay of our destination even before I looked out of the porthole of my bunk. The gentle motion of the ship riding to anchor in the bay had already told me.

At other times, it might be days before we could go in, days of sailing and tacking ship outside, waiting for winds and tide to change, days of storm that had to spend itself somewhat before we could even think of entering the Strait. These were days of impatience for all. We children were always in the cabin when gales were blowing, hearing the running scuffle of men's feet above us, the muffled shouts and orders, feeling the slap and jolt of big sails and booms shifting to the wind as the ship changed direction. Running men with lead lines taking soundings in a thick fog with no wind, running from one side to the other, fore and aft, calling out fathoms of soundings while the ship lay idle, helplessly drifting, unseeing in the white density, and over all the steady wails of foghorn hardly penetrating the white blanket that closed us in.

We nearly went aground once in such a fog. Later when Father came down to keep Mother informed he said he thought he heard breakers and told her seriously, "Close shave." Then he reported some of the readings to her. But we had drifted clear for some reason—a favorable tide or a slight puff of breeze. Later as I think back on it, I wonder how many gold pieces to Neptune had got us off? Knowing Father, I'm sure quite a few.

Ordinarily, when the weather was good and we were moving along, we sailed past Tatoosh and Neah Bay, past Clallam Bay, Port Angeles, Dungeness, Port Townsend with its many Victorian houses, and into Puget Sound to Port Gamble or Port Ludlow. We sailed through a passageway of mile upon mile of dark green trees coming down to the water's edge on both sides of us. There were endless islands, small, large, medium, all covered by trees and darkly green. To one small girl, there was never such a lovely sight or another place on earth of so many tree-covered, evergreen islands, so many tugs bustling their tows of logs. *Tyee, Goliah, Resolute, Wanderer, Pioneer, Holyoke, Sea Lion, Hercules*—mighty names for busy tugs towing ships and huge log rafts from one end of the Sound to the many lumber mills along its length and beyond.

Snow & Burgess tied up to the dock at beautiful Port Gamble with its lovely little Victorian houses and white picket fences. There were lush gardens of lilacs to be remembered each spring, and peonies and snow-

LOADING LUMBER AT PORT BLAKELY, WASHINGTON ... Five-masted *Snow & Burgess* is in the middle, taking on timber from the sawmill that hummed night and day, drawing the big logs in from the bay and cutting them into finished lumber for the many ships that crowded the wharves and each other. We could watch the burning sawdust silo, sometimes glowing red from the sawdust fed into the mill that kept the sky smoke-filled and wood-fire scented and overcast, winter and summer.

balls that burst their blossoms, covering the ground with a profusion of small petals. Wooden sidewalks clomped to small running feet . . . the whole set gem-like against a background of Douglas fir. Starting at the hotel at the rise of the hill where we climbed from the wharf, past the company store, the town—three or four blocks in length—resembled some small New

England village, ending where the forest began. In the late spring we walked whenever we could to see the tree-high rhododendrons blossoming white to pink to deepest rose and purple, to find maidenhair fern in the deep shaded places among the trees, or in summer to pick thimbleberries, wild blackberries, and strawberries to our stomach's content. When we had a horse and surrey, properly fringed on top, Mother bought berries from the farmers and made jam in the galley. In the fall we drove out for crisp juicy apples that have never seemed so sweet again.

The ship was docked near the sawmill that hummed night and day, drawing the large logs in from the bay and cutting them into finished lumber for the many ships that crowded the wharves and each other. We could watch the burning sawdust silo sometimes glowing red from the sawdust fed into it from the mill that kept the sky smoke-filled, wood-fire scented, and overcast winter and summer. We watched endlessly the bay filled with logs, the loggers riding rafts and jumping from log to log with miraculous agility, never losing their balance; directing the huge logs with long hooked poles toward the mill mouth that slowly drew them into the whirring, buzzing machinery. Tugs kept bringing more log rafts in for cutting from forests that we then thought were endless.

When we were in Ludlow we drove out to the forests in the only motor car in town. It was owned and driven by the schoolteacher, who seemed to be a bachelor, since he visited the ship alone. His name is long forgotten but not the open-top Overland he drove.

Father loved all new inventions and was endlessly curious about how the car ran and about the marvels of engines in general. He had an early Evinrude motor that he attached to one of the small deck boats when we were in port in Gamble or Ludlow. With the slightest excuse, he investigated beyond the ship's boundaries, even instigating trips around the bay to nearby islands. He also had a small sailboat and between it and the Evinrude, we did plenty of cruising around Gamble and Ludlow. Mother was never really crazy about these excursions. In the first place, the Evinrude and the sailboat put out too much speed for their size under Father's handling, so that they regularly cut sprays over the bow. In the second place, although she knew Father's reputation in handling his big ship very well, she didn't think much of his "yachting" techniques in the small craft and next-to-nothing of the Evinrude maneuvers. Sister and I never seemed to mind, not even getting a bit wet, though these trips were not too many. The sailboat and the Evinrude were ready at brief notice for trips and, in the case of the Evinrude, I suspect there was always someone on board who shared Father's enthusiasm and readily agreed to keep it oiled and cleaned in the hope of going with him in his inspections beyond the ship. Father himself was no mechanic. He had a completely equipped tool chest in museum condition for viewing and peak efficiency, but I never saw him actually use any of the tools. When we later moved ashore, Mother used them as needed, and when Father came home from sea he would oil them anew, muttering about people who failed to do so after each use.

The small enclosed bays of Port Gamble and Port Ludlow were ideal for sailing. There were many scattered islands to be explored and sandy beaches everywhere for picnics and discovery. Chief fascinations were the long ribbons of brown kelp with which we thrashed the lapping water and the tiny crabs that scooted from rock to rock. Once in a while a lifeless starfish washed up on the beach and, at low tide, myriad clam holes squirted and bubbled as we ran.

At the other end of the bay from Gamble was an Indian village, smoke rising from the clustered shacks. We never went there, but the Indians rowed in to the company store from across the bay for their trading and shopping. We saw them—quiet, dark-haired, the women with full-gathered, long cotton skirts—bringing in beaded moccasins and hand-woven baskets, some of which Father bought for us. I loved the baskets and moccasins. The Indian women with their quiet dignity and long black hair were a constant source of curiosity to small towheads. Many a day while I rowed near the ship, I looked toward the beach settlement, easily found with its lazing smoke rising, and wondered about the dark, quiet people who lived there.

Rowing. After I learned, I couldn't get enough of rowing in Sam Bagley's blue skiff, though I managed to forget that it belonged to him. Actually I was rowing in *my* boat, my own small ship, to steer, to navigate, to change course as I wanted, to explore the far

LOADING LUMBER FROM WOODEN CHUTES . . . There were several ingenius solutions to the difficult problem of loading heavy lumber and big timbers onto ship decks that were always in motion. At small doghole ports up and down the coast, wire chutes sent lumber sliding hundreds of feet down to rolling decks, made dangerous by choppy seas. It was far safer in big ports, like Port Blakely, where sling loads of lumber were drawn up wooden chutes placed over the taffrail. A steam-driven donkey engine added the much-needed hoisting power. Still, it was a dangerous job, and many a lumber coastal seaman lost a finger.

corners of the small world of water surrounding *Snow & Burgess,* while blissful hours slipped by. I don't remember how old I was when I first looked over the side of the ship and saw the beautiful blue flat-bottomed skiff. One look at the deep azure coloring, the cerulean, cloudless clime of this smallest boat tied to the float, and it was love at first sight! It *had* to be mine. I slipped down the gangway unseen, along the wharf, down another gangway to the float surrounded by other rowboats the mill hands used to row to work from across the bay. I had eyes for nothing else but the little blue boat. Looking into it, I saw neatly placed oars, the boat all clean, shipshape, and blue inside and out. I got in and pushed the boat out from the float and pulled it back a few times, leaving the painter tied as the water lapped gently against the sides. Then I tried the oars. I had an ecstatic few hours in the morning sunshine, rowing (somewhat), listening to the click of the oarlocks, the water dripping quietly from the oars back into the bay. When the dinner bell sounded at noon I hurried back to the ship. No one seemed to have missed me, so after dinner I went right back to my little blue boat.

The next morning was sunny and windless. First there was dressing and washing up and hair combing. Then breakfast with pokey adults with interminable morning amenities. Once that was over I sauntered out on deck, looked over the rail—my boat was there. In a flash I was in it again, letting the painter out to full length, rowing back and forth crookedly in the space the painter's short span allotted me. When the noon bell was heard, I scooted back on board—hungry, happy, thinking only of getting through the meal and back to the boat for the afternoon.

Halfway through the afternoon, when I was in the boat again, my glance swept the float, and there Father was standing! Wearing his dark blue suit, a hat, white shirt, hands at his sides, legs slightly apart to give him balance—his usual sea stance—looking just like he did on ship or shore when the next move could be the lightning flash of a fist that laid a seaman flat. I was struck dumb for a moment, there was no precedent for this, but only for an instant. Then he spoke, softly, "How's it going, Little Pete?"

I could relax, he'd called me Pete, his private pet name for me.

"See, I can row," I told him optimistically.

He reached down, untied the painter and threw the rope into the boat, pushing it away from the float with his foot. Then he said, "Keep the pressure even on both oars and you go straight. Now try it.

"Pull hard on the left and you go port, pull hard on the right and you go to starboard. For a complete turn around, pull hard on one oar and use the other to hold or reverse, now go to it. When you're through, be sure the boat is well tied up." Then he went back to the ship.

From then on, time in the sun was spent in my boat, first perfecting my rowing, then guiding the boat wherever I wanted to go. I even learned to feather my oars! Once this was accomplished, great explorations of the small sea and bay tides and marine life were the order of the day. I spent hours watching the clear water from the drifting boat, hanging over the stern and watching the fish swim by; moving in close to the wharf, seeing red starfish and purple mussels attached to the pilings; barnacles like tiny snow-covered volcanoes clustered on the pilings beneath the water. Sometimes Sister would appear and grant me the privilege of rowing her about, but mostly I was alone in my sheltered sea-world near the ship. It was a completely safe place for me to be: two wharves jutted out, forming a tiny bay that the ship almost completely closed off, creating approximately 75 × 100 feet of protection for me, with a small float for the six to ten boats of the mill workers who rowed to work each morning, rain or shine.

I had chosen the blue boat for my own even though blue was my sister's color. Mine was pink. It was an unvarying rule for our possessions, but I didn't expect any difficulty from her here and didn't get any. After all, why should the Little Princess bother to handle a boat when there was somebody to do it for her? Furthermore, Sister had heard it as often as I when we were off together, "Take good care of Little Sister." Anyway, Little Sister would always rather be rowed than row.

It had to have been a Sunday because we were both dressed in our starchiest, stiffest best—ruffled, dotted-Swiss, or eyelet embroidery dresses with matching petticoats and bloomers, big bows in our blonde, Dutch-cut hair, and black patent-leather, Mary-Jane shoes with long white lisle stockings. We creaked in our starchiness. For a while we wandered around the deck in the sunshine, then when the waiting got too long, I quietly left to have a quick row in my blue boat. I was happily rowing and looking at the aquarium beneath me, when I was rudely awakened from my reverie. Starchily bouffant Little Sister was on the float, demanding noisily that I take her for a row. Before someone heard the ruckus she was making, I turned my boat around and gently bumped the float, calling out to her, "Get ready to jump," and with that made a fast pivot of my boat so as to turn to present the stern of the boat for Sister to climb into. The timing here, or course, is split second for any expert competent oarsman, no matter how young. The boat was suddenly parallel to and about three feet away from the float.

Sister jumped, splashing noisily into the water, her starched finery disappearing against her small form. I remember to this day the screaming rage, the fury of her wet little face in the limp finery of her apparel. I grabbed her hand and pulled her to the gunnel of the boat and with firm strokes of the oars, tied my skiff to the float and pulled Sister up without dampening the starch of my own outfit.

By this time, Little Sister had got her second breath! All the oaths of a seaman's vocabulary streamed from her pretty little mouth; that shy little face was giving the world—even God!—a screeching show of language we weren't even supposed to know! I was sure a bolt of lightning would hit us from the sky, her for saying such things, me for knowing what she said and for letting her get wet. All that happened was the head of our first mate, Mr. Carsen, appeared over the rail of the side of the *Snow & Burgess* and he took in the situation at a glance. He started to laugh. Bellow is a better word, for he was a tall, fat man with a love of good living, and everything went into the picture he saw. The sight of Little Sister—completely drenched and dripping, screaming appropriate oaths for all the world to hear, making her wet way along the wharf—was too much. Between long laughs he managed to call to her: "Attagal, Princess, give 'em hell," before he was reduced to helpless laughter again. I'm sure when later he got back to his Philippine steamship run again, he regaled travelers at dinner with the story of Sister, the shy one whose drenching spontaneously brought out a sailor's vocabulary no one dreamed she possessed.

When we got on board after all that noise, no one was on deck! Sister marched straight into the cabin, no longer swearing, of course. I elected to stay on deck and take my chances with the lightning bolt I was sure was coming from the sunny blue sky. I waited interminably, miserably, for something to happen. It seemed hours must have passed before Sister sauntered out of the cabin, composed, hair dry, in another starched outfit not matching mine, for once, meeting me on the main deck as though nothing had happened. And still no appearance of Mother and Father. Eventually they came out, dressed to go to our Sunday visit ashore. I was very quiet the rest of the day, unobtrusive.

Many years later when Sister and I got around to talking of our childhood, her recollection of the events jibed in every respect with mine, save one. She said that I said, "Jump!" when the bow of the boat bumped the float. I maintained that I said, "Get ready to jump." Furthermore, I certainly wouldn't tell her to jump into the water! Or would I? With kids you can never be sure. Even if I had said "Jump!" it wasn't exactly bright of her to have jumped into the narrow bow of the boat, or into the bay, particularly since neither of us could swim. She never did learn; I finally learned most inexpertly at age 55. But you could never say I didn't save her small life, and single-handedly, too, when the chips were down. There certainly was a slip-up somewhere in the caring-for-Little Sister routine; however, it wasn't the last.

In looking back at a lot of these happenings, Sunday was a most likely time for them to occur. Mostly the ship was deserted, allowing for more extended explorations and more freedom to roam than on weekdays, when the ship was bustling with men and cargo. Then, too, all the tough, rough waterfront characters who comprised the main part of our small daily world were off to their normal recreational pursuits and not functioning in the fussy role of male mother hens who accepted this state of affairs as the natural role of men— men, that is, who weren't the captain.

Another Sunday had near tragic consequences and an aftermath of desperate resentment. That Sunday, too, was in lovely Port Gamble. We were having guests for the afternoon and supper in the evening. Sister and I took our brooms out on the main deck to sweep up nothing much to our heart's content. The main deck

HER DECKS MADE A FINE PLAYGROUND . . . *Snow & Burgess* was 228.5 feet long, and when we were without deckload the full length of the decks from the fo'c's'le head, including the galley and carpenter shop, up to the poop deck, were ours to roam and to explore. Coils of rope along the way were ours to play house in, or just to snuggle into in the warmth of the main deck, sheltered beneath the bulwarks. This view is a rare shot of *Snow & Burgess* in port with nothing much going on; usually her deck would be swarming with activity, loading and unloading, and we had strict orders to stay below.

was such a lovely place to play when it was free of men and cargo and swaying cranes and booms. That day we had the whole deck to ourselves, sheltered by the tall bulwarks from any breeze that might be blowing. With work stopped the hatches fore and aft were closed, hatch covers supposedly in place, covered with tarpaulins and battened down into the coamings and held in place by iron cleats. I was opposite the forward hatch when Sister climbed on top and started sweeping. Swishing her broom back and forth, she moved aft on the hatch. Then there was an unusual soughing sound. I looked up—no Sister. I moved to the hatch, looked down into the half-filled hold of lumber, which was now visible with the tarpaulin pulled away from the coaming. Little Sister was on her back on the lumber, breathless after a twelve-foot fall. Then she started to scream, still on her back with arms and legs moving in the air. The next minute, everything was utter chaos and confusion. Somehow someone came, Little Sister was brought up, someone ran ashore for the company doctor. After the doctor left, I went into the cabin. Sister was resting quietly on the sofa of the salon in the cabin. She was all right except for two shockingly large bruises, one across the shoulder blades, one on the lower back.

The guests who were spending the afternoon with us arrived as the doctor was leaving. One of the guests who was manager of the company store promptly went there and got the biggest, best doll in the store for Sister. Then, nice man that he was, he stopped long enough to pick up something for me, too—a tin-headed, black-painted-hair, unbreakable, simply dressed, sat-isfactory-under-any-other-circumstances doll. When I saw what Sister got I froze in shock and disbelief in one vast doubt in the order of the universe. This couldn't be! Things were never like this! Before this, I had known and quietly accepted the fact that I was num-

ber one child, even though everything was scrupulously equal. Presents were always the same except one
blue, one pink. We were always dressed alike even
though we were not twins. Scrupulous equity, but I
knew! And here I was receiving a vastly inferior doll!
I accepted, said, "Thank you," of course, and hated
that doll forever after. That doll took such a beating as
I never doled out to another thing in my life, then or
after. I carried her around by the feet—unheard of
treatment for dolls. With her head, I took whacks at
whatever was handy to whack. This must have been
not a steady but rather an intermittent, ongoing preoc-
cupation.

A couple of weeks later when we were at sea again,
I was in the companionway one day. Lined with ban-
nisters on both sides, the steps going up to the poop
deck were steep and edged with brass strips to steady
one's steps in pitching seas. The heavy brass strips on
the stairs were always shined by the cabin boy with
liquid metal polish applied with a cloth from the red-
covered tin can he perpetually shook. Today the brass
strips were bright, the day was fine, a steady breeze
was making the air fresh throughout the cabin—from
the open, heavy door to the deck. Usually the companionway was rather dark, but not on that day. It was a
good day to give Tin Head, the doll, her whacks at a
new locale. I whacked a low step, then a higher step,
and then Little Sister was there beside me with her
big doll. I whacked Tin Head on the next higher step,
then Sister whacked her big bisque-headed doll—but
only once, and the companionway was showered with

bisque fragments, accompanied by Sister's howls. Bob, the cabin boy, was instantly called with broom and dustpan. Order was restored in a flash, without comment. The shattered remains of Sister's doll went into the dustpan. Tin Head disappeared unaccountably a few days later. I really didn't mind but I wondered.

Anything that wasn't wanted was "deep-sixed" immediately. Davy Jones's locker must have been bulging with gold coins from the years when Father wanted to appease Neptune because there was no wind, too much wind, or wind from the wrong direction. The beautiful dappled-gray rocking horse with the real leather saddle and reins, with the gold-fringed red velvet saddle blanket that Father got for me early in life must be there, too, with many barnacles on it. Mother and Father had a terrific row over it: ridiculously expensive. I had to be put on and off the rocking horse and watched while I rode it. Mother wanted to know what was Father thinking of? Banished to the lazarete, I never saw it again. Much later I was to recall and wonder if my parents' noisy quarrel over my rocking horse was behind my lifelong fear of horses.

On another quiet Sunday morning in Port Gamble, Father greeted with particular cordiality a visitor to *Snow & Burgess*. He and the man talked awhile, then Father called us over and introduced us to the friendly Sam Bagley, owner of my blue boat. Father explained that Sam's three nephews from Seattle were visiting him in his little house across the bay and that Sam was inviting us over to spend the day with them.

Sam rowed us over in my little blue boat while Sister and I sat quiet and tongue-tied in the stern, side by side. No one talked. He rowed us across the smooth blue bay to the beach opposite, and as he neared the house, three small boys, one older than Sister and me, one younger, and one in between, came running down to the water's edge to greet the boat and Sam. Sam threw them the painter, got out, and helped them pull the boat up on the sand. Then we got out and Sam told names all around by way of introduction. Then he told us we could dig clams for dinner. This seemed to excite the two oldest boys, who ran for shovels and buckets to the single-room house standing back from the beach with smoke curling upwards from the chimney into the sunshine. Sam told us where to look for clams, gave Sister and me an example by easily digging up a couple, then left us with the boys to turn up the beach with nary a clam. The boys seemed to know more about clam-digging than we did, but their work was no more productive than ours. We dug holes, spread sand over the lower beach, scattered shovels and buckets, found ribbons of wide kelp and flayed the gently lapping water with them; we ran hollering to each other, getting hungry without even knowing it. Then Sam was ringing the bell he used to summon his nephews from wherever they might be, and we all ran toward the house.

"Time to eat," Sam said, smiling at us.

We crowded into the small unpainted room that was the house Sam lived in. The room was rather dark after the sunshine out-of-doors, but everything was orderly, stowed away compactly into place. Gray enamel cooking pots on the wall, galvanized tubs and buckets hung up and out of the way. On the cast-iron wood stove a couple of buckets were steaming from the boil, and the aroma of clams filled the place.

We huddled together on benches around the large center table, opening clams, dipping them into melted butter, stacking the shells on the table, drinking clam juice from enamel mugs, but mostly eating all the clams we wanted until we were full.

It seems odd now that I don't remember the rest of that day—what we did when we couldn't eat anymore. I don't even remember getting home. Stuffed to the gills with steamed clams, the rest of the day could have been part of an alcoholic's lost weekend for all it mattered. But whenever I get within sight or smell of steaming clams I remember the still, jewel-bright morning—the feel, the sights of the beach backed by dark green trees, topped with the heavenly fragrance of steamed clams, the memory of Sam Bagley, his little house, and his blue boat.

Port Ludlow was different from Port Gamble. Gamble was situated on a small compact bay. In Ludlow, the opposite shore was more distant and the bay more open. Ludlow itself ran uphill from the wharves, docks, hotel, and company store, along a rise overlooking the bay. Homes of the mill and store employees were built along the gently rising hill. Running parallel to it was a long beach, clean and white, with kelp and driftwood and shells. The beach is memorable for casual picnics and warm wading in shallow water, as well as the scattered treasures that we hunted assiduously along its length.

In both Gamble and Ludlow we were very friendly with the managers of the company stores and their families. I remember the Gamble store best, but not the manager's name. In Ludlow I don't remember the store so clearly, but the manager's name was Minnock, and we spent much time with his children in their big house and garden on the bluff overlooking the bay. It may possibly have been Mrs. Minnock's more modern, more relaxed attitudes toward child rearing, but Ludlow is the only place I remember going wading in my childhood, our small legs stripped of shoes and stockings behind bushes, out of sight of boys and men. We were allowed to run and wade in freedom on the open stretch of beach, but only when no boys or men were around.

Even at age 12 or 14, when we lived in Alameda after leaving *Snow & Burgess,* we went swimming in dresses that came to our knees with bloomers that filled up like balloons when we first went into the water. And we always wore long black stockings! At 15 or 16 I was allowed to buy a swimsuit all by myself and came home with an Annette Kellerman type. She was the champion swimmer who was then refusing to wear stockings for swimming and instead wore a one-piece suit not too long in the thighs. When I got home Mother took a look at it and made me try it on for her as it looked suspiciously short. Sure enough, the suit came about four inches up the thigh, and she hit the roof.

After all, it hadn't been so long since showing the ankle was considered shocking, and here was her adolescent daughter exposing her knees and quite a hunk of thigh! A younger friend of Mother's who happened to be at the house almost saved the day for me, though she laughed about that story for years after. But I didn't completely get away with it. Mother with her clever sewing techniques managed to lengthen the brief skirt before I wore it!

When we were still small, the company stores in both Ludlow and Gamble were quite large, or it seemed so to me then. They smelled of yard goods stacked in bolts to the ceiling behind the counters. Picking colors and patterns of cloth was a delight. I dreamed of dresses that could be made but I was not consulted about them. I also loved listening to the Edison and Victrola phonographs that were played all the time. The machines were rather new then, and while we had our own on the ship, it wasn't always available for listening or playing. Then, too, the stores had access to more records than we did.

Whoever hand-wound and ran the machine had a hit parade of his own selection, and number one or two on his list was Blanche Bates singing "I've Got Rings on My Fingers and Bells on My Toes" and "Cuddle Up a Little Closer, Lovey Mine." He never seemed to tire of them, and neither did I. I had the words down to memory just from listening to "Down in Jungletown, a Honeymoon is Coming Soon." We didn't have those ragtime records on the ship. They were tunes to wiggle to. Mother spent years trying to "unwiggle" us. It wasn't so easy, since we went to the Saturday night dances in Gamble and Ludlow with the grown-ups, and jazz and ragtime were everywhere.

We had many friends in both towns whom we visited and who visited us. There were the captains and their families on the ships in port. Visitors all came in hats and coats, no matter what the weather, the ladies with whole stuffed birds with glassy eyes on their hats, or just a wing or two across the top or on the sides of their big hats. Occasionally there were even ostrich feathers. All the women were tightly laced, with long-sleeved, high-necked dresses or shirtwaists and full-gored skirts that swept the ground as they walked.

Before the decade was out, women's ankles were showing with the shortening of skirt lengths, which finally ended much later when skirts reached mid-thigh!

Glimpses of things to come were provided also in that first decade of the century by the indignant disapproval of egret feathers. The lovely white feathers had to be taken by slaughtering the birds in their nests, to the near extinction of the species. Egrets, as the plumage was known, were very expensive because they could be taken only when the birds were killed while nesting in their high rocky caves. All the successful actresses had their pictures taken with egrets in their hair until a law was passed banning the slaughter. I haven't seen an egret plumage to this day, but I well remember the protest being made as I looked at pictures of them with the echoes of protest ringing in my small ear. Was this the origin of my ecological awareness?

One lovely Sunday morning in Port Gamble I went on deck after breakfast. Tied up at the end of the wharf was the biggest, most beautiful yacht I had ever seen. Gleaming white the whole length of her with varnished deck, sails tied up, and canvas awnings up over the after part of her. I watched the uniformed crew moving about for awhile and when I got tired of that, moved on to other concerns of a sunny Sunday.

Sometime after the noon dinner Mother called us in to dress. Obviously we were going ashore. When everyone was dressed we walked along the dock right to—of all things—the beautiful yacht! A couple of people were there ahead of us. The host of the little party was a very thin, actually gaunt, gray-haired man who sat in a deck chair. He did not get up from it the whole time we were there, as though he had been ill and was convalescing. Father seemed to know him quite well and the small girls were presented to the genial man. The yacht had been on a world cruise, and the men had plenty to talk about. Since the sun was comfortably over the yardarm, jacketed stewards served drinks all around. Cabin boys on the *Snow & Burgess* were jacketed, too, but the uniformed sailors on the yacht had a spit-and-polish air that contrasted sharply with the utilitarian spick-and-span shipshapeness of the crew of *Snow & Burgess*.

Then the hostess appeared from below, slim, much younger than her husband, like the beautiful young Billie Burke of the theatre magazines, her dark brown hair wound around her head in wide, flat braids. She was dressed simply, in a straight-cut, embroidered pongee with sleeves ending at the elbow, and her bare forearms were full of slim gold bracelets that tinkled as she walked. She was not laced in at the waist and, "Holy Cow!" her skirt was clear off the floor—about eight inches, with feet and ankles exposed for everyone to see.

The Isadora Duncan influence had not yet reached the West, even though she had been born in San Francisco. It had to make its way back slowly from Paris. Sister and I took one look at our hostess and bit the dust in admiration, which wasn't lost on her, I'm sure. We talked a little, then she took one of us by each hand and took us on a tour of the ship and cabin. She asked about *Snow & Burgess,* and we made comparisons. We spent the rest of the time at her side, obviously adoring her beauty and kindness, happy in the privilege of her company. Her husband and the other guests talked of the world cruise, where everybody seemed to have been. The hostess seemed to prefer our company. Looking back, I now see there was more to her than style.

Later in the afternoon we all went out from the yacht to go uptown, probably to the hotel, which was a favorite gathering spot for everyone. We did not get there. Our host stayed behind in the deck chair on board. His wife forgot something and had to go back to the yacht. While everyone waited for her, Sister and I moved away to investigate some fishermen on the wharf nearby. Two rather large crabs were on the dock amid the afternoon's catch, lying motionless with pincers wide open. With her shoe, Sister pushed the crab and got no reaction, so she reached down and put her

SAN FRANCISCO WAS HOME PORT TO *SNOW & BURGESS* . . . Before the earthquake it still had the friendly feeling of a small town, although after Port Gamble, with its lovely little Victorian houses and white picket fences, it seemed like a big city to me. Mother would take us on streetcars that left every few minutes from the Ferry Building. For five cents you could ride up Market Street and transfer to streetcars and cable cars that took you all over town.

forefinger between the pincers. She'd barely touched it when she screamed. The lifted crab told everything. Everyone came running. In a second the crab was removed and Sister had a very sore, red, swollen finger to be attended to. Father probably consulted Scammel's *Cyclopedia* and Mother proceeded to compress one small index finger of Sister's who was, for once, without benefit of whiskey, the usual "anesthesia." The crab-on-finger episode took care of the rest of the day for us from *Snow & Burgess*.

There was always plenty of coming and going while we were in port and Sister and I went along to most of it. There were Saturday night dances, Sunday school, and church, unless we had been up too late the night before. Father insisted we go to Sunday school whenever we could. As we got older, we began needling "little" Daddy to go with us, but he was always quietly firm in his refusal. Mother did not seem to mind our needling him, and stood by with an enigmatic smile and let Father handle it. He just stood with his lips pursed in a tight knot, as though words might escape that he'd be sorry for. One day when Mother had had enough of this game she said, "Your father is afraid the church would fall in on everybody if he appeared." Of course, we wouldn't want that even if we didn't understand!

In both Gamble and Ludlow I can always remember meeting the boats from Seattle. It seemed to be a midweek social gathering. The boats brought visitors and the mail, and sometimes we took the boat to Seattle. Mother did her fancier shopping at the *Bon Marche,* and we visited friends there and went to dinners of salmon and oysters and clam chowder in the fish restaurants along the waterfront. We two well-behaved little girls went along to everything so when it came time to visit the *Glenwood* we went along to that, too.

We had passed the *Glenwood* while in Ludlow, on our walks up the hill to the Minnock house. It was probably from the Minnock children that we had picked up the buzzings of sin and scandal that hung over the house. We never failed to stare at this quiet, well-kept Victorian, white-painted, and picket-fenced house, which looked like the rest of the houses that presented an air of solitude. The *Glenwood* was occupied by one Kenneth Stuart, a bachelor, who was reported to be the "very old Nick" with half the women in town. When an invitation came to spend an evening at the *Glenwood,* Father and Mother had one of their incomprehensible rows. Mother was full of her best indignation and Father, as usual, scoffed. It all had something to do with red lights in the parlor, which sounded rather nice to me though I'd never known anyone else who used them. But Mother was exhibiting her best Victorian attitude. Father was also a Victorian, but one of those "Other Victorians" of whom Steven Marcus writes. Father had been born and raised in Copenhagen, and as a child played around the docks and ships and fishing boats that surrounded the city. From an early age he had been a part of, or at least had observed, activities that all humans at all levels left free to roam are exposed to. There was not much of the world of men he did not know and he had long ago made his choices.

Imagine my surprise when one evening we walked along the broad sidewalk that adjoined the picket fences and turned into the *Glenwood* and rang the bell. The interior of the house was friendly and darkly warm, with red carpets and velvet drapes and the glow from red lampshades from the tables beside the red Victorian chairs. In the center of the room lay a large, thick, white bearskin rug with glassy-eyed head and snarling, red-felt, wide-open, wickedly toothed mouth. We small girls succumbed to the obvious and threw ourselves down on the rug. To Mother's horrified, "Get up," Mr. Stuart, the host, complacently answered, "Perfectly all right. Let them alone," and since there were others present, there the matter was left. We soon relaxed into the sensuous luxury of the rug and fell asleep. We only visited the *Glenwood* that once, but of all the houses we ever visited, *Glenwood* was the most memorable, the sharpest memory of any house of our childhood. I wonder how much of this was due to the aura of refined, high-class sin that hung over it?

3

*Should Auld Acquaintance Be Forgot
and Never Brought to Mind . . . .*

Scottish Folk Song

FATHER sailed a smoothly run ship. Everything all shipshape from paint work to masts to deck. All brass gleaming on deck instruments; good meals were served on time; clean, comfortable cabins ready for visitors at all times. Naturally, with such requirements it was necessary to have a first-class crew, as far as Father was able to pick one. He didn't want any "Philadelphia lawyers" in the fo'c's'le, nor anyone with a "bad eye" or "slow to get a move on" when the situation might call for quick action. Father knew a "bad eye" when he saw one—at sight—and knew he'd have trouble. "Philadelphia lawyers" were of another kind. They were followers of that "bad actor" Andrew Furuseth who was agitating for reform of sailors' conditions by forming a union. Father, who hand-picked his crew and usually got a good one, was all for the status quo of sailors the world over and didn't want a "radical" like Furuseth to come along and upset things.

Father died in 1938, before the statue of Andrew Furuseth was erected at the foot of Market Street in

San Francisco, and accolades were given to him, almost in awe. Knowing the whole history of the sailors' condition at first hand, Father had changed in agreement with the need and the times, for by the middle 1930's, he had done picket duty himself with Master, Mates, and Pilots in their first strike. But, in my early seafaring days Andrew Furuseth was a "dangerous radical."

Nevertheless, the sailors union agents were always courteously received and welcomed on *Snow & Burgess*. Frequently there were meals and drinks. I'm sure, knowing my father, that there were also payoffs on the q.t. Father always greased wheels so they wouldn't squeak, and as far as he was concerned red tape was something to cut his way through in advance. The result was that he always had a crew at a moment's notice. If he had more time, he selected more carefully, but nothing—not even strikes—ever kept him from sailing on schedule. The date and time of sailing were ordained by God, the ship's readiness, and the tides, and the captain was not bucking Fate. Sometimes, crews of sailors walked off the ship. The length of time it took Father to contact the sailors' union agent was precisely the length of time we were delayed. The new crew may not have been hand-picked, there may have been a "bad eye" or two or more of the slower-moving among them, but there was always the next port to pay them off in, only about two weeks away. For two weeks he could cope with just about anything.

The mates, carpenter, cook, and cabin boy were pretty much permanent fixtures. From trip to trip they all remained, except for an occasional layoff. Shimoda,

the cook, had a family in Japan to be visited from time
to time. Then the carpenter, Carl Holmstrom, unaccountably disappeared from our lives one day and we
never heard of him again. He was replaced by another
big and blond Swede, Charlie Bolond, who walked
with an exaggerated rolling gait and was always good-
natured and grinning. Father liked Charlie Bolond, as
we all did, but he never became the love of our lives
that Carl had been. Perhaps it was because we were
bigger, but I suspect the manner of Carl's leaving had
something to do with it.

Shimoda, the cook, was there from our earliest
memory until after we went to school. He left only for
his trips to Japan to see his family, and he returned
again when his wife got pregnant. He was a lovely
guy, mostly quiet and earnest and kindly, and very
patient, unless pushed too far, poor soul. Cookie, as
we used to call him—or in more needling moments,
Little Cookie—put up with us underfoot as he worked
hard all day preparing meals for the cabin and fo'c's'le,
and between-meals and night snacks for the whole crew.
I'm sure he'd have preferred my sister and me elsewhere a good deal of the time, but when Father
appeared and asked, "Are the girls bothering you, Shimoda?" he answered, "No, no bother." It was no bother
to bake mince pie in July because it was Little Sister's
favorite and she'd asked for it. So, everybody ate mince
pie even if it was warm July. Once, though, there were
disastrous results, to Sister's and Shimoda's distress.
The quantity consumed and a roughish sea put the

whole thing on deck and Sister to bed for a couple of hours.

The galley was a fascinating place to be. There was always a fire going in the big iron galley range, roaring or banked. All sorts of pots and pans were hanging from hooks, and there were drawers full of interesting utensils. Bins were full of flour and oatmeal, which Shimoda cooked very slowly day and night for the morning breakfast. There was a coffee grinder, a coffee pot, and freshly roasted coffee that was always boiling and ready for use.

The galley was open on both sides, weather permitting, with sliding doors to be used as needed. It was warm and light, good smelling, and immaculately clean. There was a small stateroom adjacent on the port side with two bunks for cook and cabin boy. The carpenter's room with one bunk was in the same position on the starboard side.

When the main meal at noon was over and the cooking utensils all cleaned and put away, Shimoda took a much-needed rest and sometimes slept. We had been told repeatedly not to bother Shimoda, so we used to slip into the galley very quietly and set to work making mud pies. But here there was no mud, only flour, which had to do until the real stuff came along. We made the most of what we had and went to work happily sloshing water into flour. Sometimes, in our intense play, in an unguarded moment, we dropped a spoon or bowl or a pan, or got into a noisy argument and then the jig was up. Shimoda was out of his bed, holding his head with both hands, screaming his "Jesus Christ, Jesus Christ, my galley, my galley." He always began by cursing everything in English and then lapsing into incomprehensible Japanese. When he'd recovered sufficiently to talk coherently, he said: "Go now, I clean up. Little Cookie will clean up for you, go now. I tell Captain. Captain my friend."

Shimoda always spoke as though he thought the captain would settle everything from on high. We left uncomprehending, because the captain was our friend, also, and why anyone should ask him to threaten us was always a mystery. Anyway, Father wasn't apt to be around when friend Cookie needed him any more than when we did. Another variation of this situation was, "Go see Carpenter," who wasn't really his enemy, although you might think so, just casually looking over the situation. Now, if the poor, misguided creature had only said, "Go, now, I tell your Mother," he might have had something. But this never seemed to occur to him or to anyone. "I'll tell the Captain" seemed to be the ultimate authoritative statement, and for the crew it was. So this is what they used if they used anything, which was generally unlikely.

Mother had a fiery temper and no trouble making decisions regarding the girls. One bang from the flat of her hand, and she was through with the matter. We were, too. But Father, on the other hand, struggled with frustration when it came to disciplining us. Sometimes when he thought we weren't around, he'd come storming into the cabin and holler at Mother, "Can't you make those girls behave?" Mother would answer, looking up comfortably from her reading or sewing, "Why don't *you* make them?" Then if he saw us, he'd turn on his heel and go on deck. The better part of valor for him seemed to be in getting lost, which he did most easily. Mother's sphere seemed to cover us and our outbursts, which she dealt with directly. Father's sphere was the ship and its domain. She never interfered with his domain.

The next time we saw Shimoda he would have cookies for us. When we saw Father again he seemed to have forgotten, too. But that was the way with adults—hollering unreasonably, irrationally one minute, than as nice as pie or cookies the next.

When Shimoda was off on his occasional trips to Japan, there were only two replacements. One was a portly Chinese cook, quiet and dignified on the ship, but not on shore leave. He always returned to the ship roaring, grandly drunk, like some Chinese emperor shedding his largess among the peasants. At such times we learned about lichee nuts, crystalline coconut and melon strips, and dry, sugared ginger. Another time Father signed on a Jamaican Negro named Lazarus as cook and his white, cockney English wife as "cabin boy," a miscegenation many years ahead of the times. Lazarus was without doubt a most refined and intelligent, dignified person. I see and hear him still, with his gentle and handsome expression and his crunchy, musical Jamaican accent. I always recall him when I hear Calypso singers. Mrs. Lazarus was neurotically sensitive and forever in tears, scarlet-faced most of the time clear to her toes, I'm sure, from remarks the sailors made as she passed them on deck. In no time my Mother had become her confidante and taken up the cudgels in her defense, and also in no time Mother had to agree with Father that steward Lazarus was one fine person. You only had to look at him once to know. But when Mother complained to Father about the sailors making remarks as Mrs. Lazarus passed, he only asked, "What do you expect me to do? I never see anything out of the way when *I'm* on deck."

Lazarus was excellent in the galley, and Mrs. Lazarus was doing a good job as "cabin boy" in spite of being red-eyed and red-faced most of the time, and the sailors were circumspectly doing their duties. All seemed serene to Father's eye although, without being told, he undoubtedly must have known the sailors' attitudes. Later, in Alameda, Lazarus and his wife came to visit us; Father had invited them when he'd run into them somewhere or other in his travels. They spent an afternoon and had dinner with us, as all friends from the ship did.

One of the bright shining memories of our life was Carl "Carpie" Holmstrom—the big, blond, curly-haired, ripply-muscled, good-natured Swede. For us he was fascinating. He went about the hot carpenter shop with its fired-up donkey engine doing his work, the upper half of him naked and glistening and rippling with every move. Father was never like this, always buttoned to the neck and wrists no matter how hot the weather. We were practically grown before we discovered the mysterious tattoos on Father's arms and chest. It was quite by accident, and only after much discussion and needling did we see them for a moment. The buxom lady in the low-cut gown, the heart with the arrow through it, dripping drops of blood on his chest, the wing-spread eagle waving an American flag from his claws. On his right hand was an anchor with A.H.S., his initials, below in a conservative blue. The other tattoos were flamboyantly colored.

Carpie, however, wasn't tattooed. It wasn't long before we'd taken to watching him for himself, alone— muscles all rippling nakedly as he reached and pulled and hammered and planed at his work in the hot shop, reaching for a piece of cotton waste to wipe the sweat from his face or remove oil from his hands. When he planed he made lovely curls for the straight-haired little girls, and we were underfoot retrieving the longest. While Carl rested sitting on the floor, we were on either side of him with small hands clasped around the biceps of his arms. He would clench each big fist and our hands would burst off his biceps to our noisy giggles. Then Father's head would appear in the doorway.

"The girls bothering you, Chips?"

"Oh, no, just resting."

"Well, don't bother Chips, girls."

"Oh, no, we won't."

In fair weather at sea, when the ship was empty, hatch covers were removed and a heavy ladder was placed into the after hold from the opening. Carpie, with his big tool kit, used to go below into the 'tween decks. Had the big ship sprung a leak and the Captain wanted to know the extent of it? No matter. Boats were always springing leaks, so unless it was very bad no one paid any attention to it. If there was too much water in a boat you used a can to bail, but on *Snow & Burgess* you started up the donkey engine and pumped ship when the bilges were too full of water. When you got to port you went into the dry dock, which was also interesting with the ship sitting a long way up in the air and no water about you, and when you wanted to get off to go ashore you went down a long ladder.

Why Carpie went below to the ballasted empty hold was not important to us, but simply *that* he went below was. It meant we could go too, so with Carpie, down we went.

Once we took our cat with us into the hold. Immediately below she shot off into the darkness. We heard a squeak and she sauntered back with a mouse between her teeth, went toward the ladder, and carefully made the rungs up to the main deck. Fascinating. How could Kitty see in the black hold, where we could see nothing?

Just going below with Carpie was not to be missed. As Carpie moved away from the light coming through the hatch openings, he would light tall white tallow candles to search the cavernous gloom. The sound of the sea against the empty hull made a different rhythm from the sea topside. He searched the sides of the ship and gave us each a candle, too, and taught us to make wax drippings to set them on when we wanted to be free to get to Carpie's tool kit. With a plane, a saw, and a hammer, nails, and pieces of wood, we began to play.

After awhile, Father would appear.

"How's it going, Chips? What did you find?" he would ask.

While Carpie explained, we girls were busy with our constructions.

"How long do you think this will take, Chips?" Father would ask drily.

"Oh, it looks like it's going to be quite a while."

"Looks that way to me, too. Well, take your time."

As far as anyone knew Carpie never took a drink. Certainly he never went off on the big payoff binges most of the men did. And possibly his leaving had nothing to do with drink. Whatever it was it left all of us with painful, aching memories for years after, and for me, grief in the loss of an early affection.

I'll always remember the quiet Sunday in Port Gamble, a sunny, smoke-hazed day smelling of the perpetually burning sawdust of the huge, waste wood-burning silos of the mill. *Snow & Burgess* was deserted and I was on the poop deck lazing at the rail, watching the moods and changes of the water. Suddenly Carpie was on the ship roaring for the Captain. Without further warning, he ran up on the poop deck, and when Father came up to him, Carpie's fists struck out and both men went down rolling on the deck on top of each other, with fists flying in all directions. I'd seen Father in fights before. He was never down. Usually it was one or two clips and the fight was over, but not this time. The two men rolled over and over, punching and slugging, while I stood by torn in two directions. Father always won, he *had* to win, but Carpie couldn't lose, either. Suddenly, both men were up, and while Father watched, Carpie went down the steps to the main deck forward into his room in the carpenter shop. Father went below. I stayed on deck looking toward the fo'c's'le. In a little while Carpie reappeared with duffel bag over one shoulder and tool box in the other hand. He walked off the ship and I watched him disappear up the dock. When Father came out again I told him Carpie had gone. Father didn't say anything then, but he fussed over the happening many times and confessed to Mother, "He nearly had me. If he hadn't been drunk I couldn't have handled him." He wondered repeatedly what had happened. Father thought he knew Carpie; he certainly liked him. But why? I think he finally satisfied himself that Carl was one of those people who just couldn't drink. This seemed a reasonable explanation to him. But to me, it remained a puzzling, nagging memory, and a loss of an early affection that I remembered when reading John Masefield's lines:

> *Man cannot call the brimming instant back;*
> *Time's an affair of instants spun to days;*
> *If man must make an instant gold, or black,*
> *Let him, he may, but Time must go his ways.*
> *Life may be duller for an instant's blaze.*
> *Life's an affair of instants spun to years,*
> *Instants are only cause of all these tears.* *

Sometimes a selected sailor would take us fishing on the Sound on a quiet Sunday. Father himself wouldn't

---

* From "The Widow in the Bye Street" by John Masefield.

have been caught dead rowing a small boat so we could fish, but it was easily arranged with certain sailors and worth the man's while, I'm sure, knowing Father. One Sunday we went quite a way from the ship, then threw in the line with hook and silvery, swiveling spoon on the end of it, trolling for salmon on the gentle bay. Sister was in the bow watching the waters about her, I was in the stern handling the fishing line, the sailor was on the oars rowing like crazy. The faster he rowed, the more sparkly the silver lure with hook beneath it spun and twisted just under the water. We went on for some time; then what looked to me like a silver whale leaped to the hook! I started to holler for help, standing up in the boat, everything jiggling and rocking, but before the sailor could place his oars and carefully come to help, the silver salmon had freed itself, leaping in all directions, and was gone. I was grief-stricken. The sailor tried to console me: "We'll try again, only this time, stay down, keep the line tight when it strikes."

We rowed around for what seemed ages but no more salmon were to be seen. Finally we went back to the ship. When we got on deck Father and Mother were there with some visitors, perhaps six or eight in all. In great excitement I told them, "I caught a salmon—this big—but it got away." In unison, everybody broke into gales of laughter. All my protests and the sailor's, "Yes, sir, she did," were of no use. Everybody had a big, noisy laugh. They hurt my little feelings and I didn't understand the whole thing, anyway. It was to be many years before I heard the comfortable retort of the fisherman: "This is nothing. You shoulda seen the one that got away."

There were times afterward when I've wondered if, in picking a crew, Father's aim was not only to choose a complement of competent A.B.'s—the ship *had* to run and the men *had* to know their business—but also men who could be made into nannies or surrogate, part-time male mothers of the most patient kind. These sailors came in an international assortment—Scandinavians, "Rooshin-Finns," Portuguese, Spanish, French, Limeys—with all the tongues and shades of male maternity from bored acceptance of the role to real concern and watchfulness, with an indulgence of gifts—carved ships in small bottles, wooden animals, and red heart boxes of chocolates on pay day. They never seemed to have families, and perhaps we girls awakened memories of other ties, other days, other places.

We accepted ourselves as part of the crew, and tugboat skippers both in San Francisco and on the Sound recognized this by calling through the megaphone to Father as they came alongside: "How're your first and second mates?" Women's lib had a big start in that first decade of my life with Father.

Of all the crew members, my most tender memories belong to Bob Wakamea, the cabin boy. He was playmate, protector, and teacher. He signed on while still an adolescent: when he left the ship to go to Alaska to make his fortune he was still a young man, though he'd been on the ship several years.

Mother and Father agreed they had a jewel in Bob. He got on well with Shimoda, which made for good

CAPTAIN SORENSON (FAR LEFT) WITH CREW . . . The mates, carpenter, cook, and cabin boy were pretty much permanent fixtures. From trip to trip they all remained, except for an occasional layoff. Shimoda, the cook, had a family in Japan to be visited from time to time. I've wondered if, in picking a crew, Father's aim was not only to choose a complement of competent A.B.'s—the ship *had* to run and the men *had* to know their business—but also they were men who could be made into nannies or surrogate, part-time male mothers of the most patient kind.

working conditions in the galley. He certainly got along well with everyone in the cabin. My sister and I could frequently be found hanging onto Bob with both hands, as he made trips between the galley and cabin loaded with dishes or water, dragging our small feet along with his racing stride. Sometimes we hung from a broom he held over his shoulders. Because he was young and strong and liked to play too, none of this ever seemed to bother him.

Best remembered of Bob was his role as retriever of floating brooms and soggy dolls that Sister heaved to Davy Jones's locker. While in midair she changed her mind about their destination, and howled heartbrokenly to have them back as she watched them float away. The first time this happened was a quiet day of sailing, when she tossed a rag doll overboard. Father altered the ship's course and lowered a boat with two men to row and Bob to retrieve. By the time the ship had 'scribed a slow arc about them, Bob and the boat and the two rowers had met the ship, were hauled back on board, and the ship was on course again. Not too much trouble, really. A few men involved, a small amount of time lost, but big excitement for two small girls. I remember being terribly impressed, maybe even a tinge jealous. I knew I'd never do that to a doll that I cared for. No gambler I, but I could enjoy the spectacle on an otherwise uneventful day. On periodic dull days in Gamble or Ludlow when Sister hurled a broom or doll over the rail, then bawled as befitting the sad occasion, Bob would strip off his outer garments and shoes, and in his long johns dive into the water of the bay and swim around, retrieving the broom. He would climb up the rope-and-wood ladder that was lowered for him, up the side of the ship, and in a matter of minutes, Sister was back in business with her wet broom, sweeping the deck as she had been when the broom had "inadvertently" slipped out of her little hands.

About the third time this happened, Father was looking askance at the wisdom of his action in turning the ship around. Sister should learn that anything thrown overboard should be regarded as gone forever. But how to handle the situation? Turning a ship around at sea wasn't always possible, not even for a "man overboard" signal. Wild winds, mountainous seas, clipper-speed knots lost anything or anyone in a matter of minutes, as Father well knew. A sticky problem of child discipline. Meanwhile, Bob went right ahead with his Johnny-on-the-spot strips and dives after Little Sister had indulged her heaves and howls. Mostly the whole thing was over before you could stop it. And so it went on until Callao. We spent a lot of time watching these murky waters, thickly opaque, turbid, yellow, so different from the waters of the sound. Then one day the broom was floating again, Sister was howling. Bob was there. Then there was Father. He was talking to Bob very quietly and firmly. Bob, very earnest, quiet, and respectful, was protesting. Arguing with Father! I couldn't hear what they were saying but I could see what was happening. I couldn't believe my eyes. Finally Father turned on his heels and walked away. Bob stripped and dove, and Sister's broom was saved.

What had the quiet argument been about? That it was time Little Sister learned about things overboard? That the murky waters might be, possibly were, shark infested? That Father didn't want to lose his favorite cabin boy to them? The toss-howl habit had to wait another day. The whole game ended on the harsh reality which the situation called for without Father's ever having to confront the problem or knowing what happened. For all he ever knew Little Sister had taken a leap from a learning plateau and left the whole pattern behind. But that's not quite what happened.

One afternoon, on the homeward return to Puget Sound, a stiff breeze sent the ship scudding to maximum knots with all sails, jibs, tops'ls full and steady. It was a beautiful day, Sister began "One for the money, two for the show, three to get ready, and four to go." With "four" the doll went flying over the rail. Before she'd even had a chance to work up a wail, Mr. Hansen, the mate who was on deck with us, exploded, "Jesus Christ, now you've done it!" And indeed she had. The doll was so far astern it disappeared immediately. Only one look was needed to tell us. Sister wasn't even crying. She was more surprised and stunned at what an unassessed survey of the facts could bring about. She'd also have to wait until we got to port for another doll. For all it was an unsettling affair; anticlimactic, a nothingness from being, even with Mr. Hansen's explosion. Evidently the whole situation was serious enough for her to think about. It never happened again.

Sister or I never thought of Mr. Hansen as being among our friends in the way that Cookie, Carpie, and Bob were our friends. But I think that he was, nevertheless. When Father was not around Mr. Hansen was, and although he seemed dull and uninteresting, he saved my neck on occasion, as when I scratched up the newly painted bitts on the poop deck. Chipped down properly as all iron work was, covered with layer after layer after layer of red lead, the bitt was a beautiful thing to behold with its curved shiny surface that was not thoroughly dry and hard from a new coat. I admired it for awhile, then got a heavy nail from some convenient source and went to work gouging out careful straight lines down to the iron, then crossing them so there were even squares on the whole top. I was admiring my handiwork when Mr. Hansen came by and exploded, "Jesus Christ, now you've done it. This time I can't save you."

He promptly went off for some red lead and a brush and patiently began filling the cracks I had made. I watched for awhile, wondering guiltily how I could have lapsed so far from good judgment as to practice my Mondrian inspiration on a ship's bitt. Then I left Mr. Hansen to his muttering chore. Later, when I returned, I casually sauntered by. Mr. Hansen was gone but the checks were not, although the cracks were filled with as much red lead as they could hold. Father would surely see that I had been practicing decorating in the wrong place. What would happen? With no precedent for such a singular incident, I could only wonder. Every time I passed the bitt, a glance told me the whole story was screaming for recognition. Strangely, Father never seemed to see it, for all his eagle-eyed renown. The checks stayed for quite a long time, and I learned to live with them. Apparently Father did, too, although it was a more difficult choice for him: chip down the whole bitt, or just not notice the whole thing. Father chose to ignore it.

Although I don't remember it, there was an evening walk in heavy dew which Mother told us about gleefully in after years. Fresh, white, wet paint work was all over the wheel housing, heavily dotted with dew, and we two girls were walking with the family and first mate. As we got to the wheel housing, we jumped up on it then off, and continued our walk. Mr. Hansen quickly wiped off the foot marks with his bandana. Mother watched. Father gave no sign of hearing or seeing anything.

I'm sure we just took Mr. Hansen's unobtrusive care for granted, so imagine my surprise when one day he came out of his room with a toy piano under his arm and said I could have it if I gave him a kiss. Quandary of quandaries, what to do? If there was one thing (and there was more than one) that Mother absolutely laid down the law on, it was no kisses given to or received from anyone on the ship. Make no mistake about that! So I told Mr. Hansen, "Mother says we can't." Slyly, Mr. Hansen countered: "Well, I'll see if your sister will." Right there I died on the spot. Suppose she did? I'd lose the beautiful piano, and Sister would be tinkling the wooden ivories of its 15-inch keyboard. I'd be hearing but not touching it, and dying of the poison of green-eyed jealousy in its most virulent form. All to be borne for the loss of one small kiss. I was sitting on the floor of the dining room with the piano before me. Suddenly I made one of Father's instant decisions: I kissed Mr. Hansen softly on the cheek, and grabbed the piano under my arm and fled into the cabin.

In later years when I thought of Mr. Hansen and remembered—clearly, very clearly—the episode of the piano, I really wondered. Mr. Hansen was a most unprepossessing man, always in dull, dark clothes, quiet to the point of being speechless except for deck orders. If he drank, and I think he did, it was alone and in his room and it never interfered with his duties. He carried out Father's wishes like clockwork and had his chief's backing to the hilt. An excellent first mate for Father's exacting needs, but socially, even to a small girl, he was a thin, dark wraith with holes in him. I had this one small glimpse of a person with needs and wants like everyone else, but after this one glimpse, I never had another. He was with *Snow & Burgess* for many years and when he left, it was as though he'd just disappeared, and no one seemed to notice.

Mr. Hansen's replacement, Mr. Carson, was a direct opposite in every way. Mr. Carson was a tall, portly sophisticate with an aura of well-being that lasts to this day. He had a lust for life and its finest goods. He came to *Snow & Burgess* under a cloud of sorts. He had been a steamboat officer in the Philippines who'd had his papers revoked or gotten into some scandal, perhaps with women. I never really knew. But he'd come to San Francisco, needing a job, and Father needed a mate and apparently couldn't be bothered about the circumstances. Anyway, whatever the cloud, it was something Father understood, and the two men hit it off from the start.

Mr. Carson had class, make no mistake about it. First, there were the white suits he'd worn on the Manila run. They were not the pressed, starched whites of his standing, but more casually worn unofficerlike garments. They nonetheless reminded everyone of their former function, even without insignia. Second, there was the change of atmosphere at mealtime. Mr. Carson was accustomed to much and lively conversation, laughter, and pleasantries. Quite different from the diffident presences of former mates. A year later, after serving his banishment period on *Snow & Burgess,* he left. He was missed by all of us and remembered vividly by Sister and me. He was the witness to Sister's near "drowning" and pyrotechnic swearing in Port Gamble.

As I dredge up these memories, there seem to be so many sharp outlines of unforgettable people, but the clearest and warmest memory is of Bob Wakamea. Bob stayed with the ship until we left to go to school in the fall when Sister was seven and I was eight. Then Bob set off for the gold fields in Alaska to make his fortune. He would come to see us when he got back, rich. And so he left. We were busy with the excitement of school and a new life ashore, and it wasn't until later that Father had news of Bob in Alaska—he had fallen asleep in the snow and frozen to death. Father said, "It is an easy thing for newcomers to Alaska to do. You just get drowsy with the cold, sit down to rest, and go to sleep.

There is no pain. You never know." Perhaps this was Father's way of softening our pain.

For this loveliest memory out of my childhood, a beautiful place in some celestial paradise to you, dear Bob—*i tid og evighed.**

* *Danish:* Through all eternity.

We Pointed Her Nose toward a Souther-en Star[*]

THE trip *Snow & Burgess* made to South America began differently from other trips. In the first place, the ship was towed by tug from Pope & Talbot's lumber yard in San Francisco, where we usually were based, to Oakland Long Wharf for loading. Gone these many years now, the old wharf was built in the early part of the state's history and jutted out from the Oakland mole—also gone now to make room for a BART (Bay Area Rapid Transit) section. The Oakland mole was for many years the terminus for passenger and freight trains that covered the continent. The long wharf has been gone since 1918, but when we loaded a cargo of lumber for South America in the first decade of the century, it jutted an incredible two miles into San Francisco Bay. Cargoes were carried along the wharf on railroad trains and tracks, to ships loading and unloading along its sides.

Trains and tracks along the wharf right next to the

---

[*] From the traditional sea chantey, "Way Rio."

OAKLAND LONG WHARF JUTTED TWO MILES INTO SAN FRAN-
CISCO BAY . . . *Snow & Burgess* started her trip to South America
from this wharf. Unlike San Francisco, the tracks and trains came
right out into the bay to meet the ships on this causeway. Oakland
had an early monopoly on the transcontinental railroad freight
business that was always a sore point with San Francisco. In 1896,
San Francisco challenged Oakland's early advantage with the Belt
Line Railroad that made a continuous circuit of her waterfront, but
there was no way the city could match her rival's enormous railroad freight and waterfront shipping combination.

ship were a totally new experience for Sister and me.
It was Sunday and all the surrogate male mothers were
off on their Sunday business (which did not include
church) and freed from their watch of two small girls.
We were free to quietly explore the tracks. We slipped

down the gangway and soon were balancing on the tracks like tight-rope walkers. We were balancing ourselves pretty skillfully on either side of the tracks when a locomotive ahead whistled and startled us. We jumped. At least, I did. Sister had been on one of those rail off-shoots used for changing directions from one track to another. When she jumped she got her foot stuck in the crack of the rails and couldn't get it out.

"Take good care of Little Sister!"

I pulled and pulled on the small foot and she wailed and wailed. The locomotive kept whistling at us to get off the tracks, all the time coming slowly toward us. Were we both to die on the tracks? Would anyone save us? Unknowingly we anticipated by several years that moment when the movie screen message said, "To be continued next week"—to find out what happened to *The Perils of Pauline* that we would watch breathlessly every Saturday matinee at the Lincoln Theatre in Alameda. But I couldn't wait for next week! The train kept moving toward us breathing smoke from its stack. Then inspiration struck me! I unlaced Sister's shoe. Unlaced from the shoe, the foot came right out—and miracle of miracles, the shoe came, too, eliminating the need for an explanation of the missing shoe. I grabbed it, and Sister and I raced back to the safety of the ship. Once on deck, she put on her shoe and I laced it. Nobody had even missed us!

We finished loading at Oakland Long Wharf. The hold was full of lumber but the decks were free of cargo both outward and homeward bound so that the whole

Unloading at Pope & Talbot Lumberyard . . . From Mission
Creek south, as far as the eye could see, all was stacks and stacks
of open lumberyards. *Snow & Burgess* picked up a Red Stack tug
near Meiggs Wharf, off North Beach, to maneuver the big ship
into China Basin and along the north side of Mission Creek where
her cargo was unloaded. On Sundays, when the lumber wharf was
deserted, the lumber piles made lovely playhouses. We played house
with a waterfront view of the bay, and sometimes rainbow spills of
oil that changed shape and color with gently lapping water.

length of the ship was free to roam—both ways through
the tropical weather.

Once loaded, the trip began as all trips did from San
Francisco. A Red Stack tug towed us out on the ebb
tide, past the familiar rows of docks with their tangle
of masts silhouetted against the city, through gulls

wheeling and screaming and diving overhead, through the Golden Gate, past Mile Rock Lighthouse with its mournful wail of foghorn that sometimes sounded like the heavy snoring of a sleeping giant. Past the Lightship, then the Farallones, to drop hawser when we were clear of land and all sails were set.

Father never sailed on Friday, or the 13th, and most certainly never on Friday the 13th! Father—and I'm sure the whole crew to a man—would have jumped ship rather than court disaster in this way. Father had never had an accident to his ship and he was keeping the record clean. Many seamen knew this as well as knowing that a ship had ghosts. Father used to see the ghost of one of *Snow & Burgess's* former skippers as he walked the moonlit decks late at night. He was sure of this, but he was never able to discuss it with a liberated scoffer like Mother who'd never seen a ghost and wouldn't have believed they existed. When she tried to question him about the ghosts he claimed he'd seen, Father just drew his mouth together tight and refused to answer, silently calling on whatever amendment or article protected seamen from scoffers.

Once on our way to South America, it wasn't many days before we knew something was different. Sea and wind were subtly changed, gentler. There began to be warmer sunshine and more of it. *Snow & Burgess* settled into easy rhythmic sailing. Evenings, Sister and I with Father began to watch for the first star of the Southern Cross to show. We watched until all four stars were clear in the heavens, and nightly we watched it move north across the sky. Homeward bound, we watched the process in reverse as star by star dropped over the horizon and disappeared, to be gone except in memory. No need to be told when we went to school that the world was round, we'd seen it.

I think it must have been on the South American trip that we first started looking over the weather side from the fo'c's'le head. Father took us there for the first time to see a whale breaching the smooth waters, blowing and sounding, waving a huge triangle of tail as it disappeared into the ocean. Father left us there, with the necessary precautions, to watch for more whales. After that, I was a regular visitor to the fo'c's'le head. It was the most ideal place on the whole ship for an unobstructed view, the highest place except for the mastheads. I could sit on the dock, lean over the rail, and look out. Long after the last black fluke had slipped back into the sea, I stayed and watched; I leaned over the bulwarks for hours and endlessly followed the ship's prow as it cut its course through the sunshine of the deep blue waters.

One day dolphins were there, swimming just below the surface, close to the ship, and leaping in joyful play, many of them crisscrossing all around us, now in the air, now underwater, measuring their speed to ours. When they left us, the dolphins sped away many times faster than the ship. This was the first of many such memorable visits from these friendly marine animals that no sailor would dream of harming. Father was full of the lore of dolphins, all confirmed for me when I got into high school and Greek mythology.

It was around this time we first saw flying fish in

schools, leaping ahead of us, their gossamer wings seeming to glide them into an aerial ballet. Beautiful things to see and some of them landed on deck. Shimoda picked up the small, foot-long length of fish and spread out the stiff wings for us to see, then he cooked them for us for dinner. I don't remember eating them myself and perhaps I didn't. The small, sparkling visions from the sea did not seem for eating like some mundane mackerel.

One day, before we hit the doldrums and while the wind still held, the sailors had to hoist sails. I'd seen them do this before but I'd never heard sails hoisted to rollicking sea chanteys. The first words come back to me as clearly as the first time: "As I was a-walking down Paradise Street, singing, 'Way, aye, blow the man down,' a pretty young maiden I chanced for to meet, give me some time to blow the man down." All the while they sang they pulled together, swaying in rhythm with the pull of the rope and all joining in on the chorus, "Blow the man down, Bullies, blow the man down, give me some time to blow the man down."

Sister and I ran out on deck to watch and listen until the sails were fully up. Before the trip was over we had learned "Whiskey for My Johnnie," "Way Rio," and the hauntingly beautiful "Shenandoah"—one of the most poignant melodies ever written.

No one ever explained to me how we got sea chanteys on this trip. Most likely it was the crew of deep-water sailors as opposed to the coast-wise crew we usually had. There were other differences, too, like the sailors' hobby of making knots in fine cord, producing gifts for us in what is now fashionable as macramé. They also made picture frames of cut-out layers of thin wood, alternating and lacquered in natural or dyed colors. Some made ships in bottles, others picture frames of paste waves and half ships in calm relief. When the trip was over, a sailor gave me a three-foot long model of a three-masted schooner with sails that lowered and set and booms that had small blocks and tackles and a wheel that turned the rudder. All of this rested in a wooden frame.

Sailing into warmer waters brought us other wonders and reduced the ship's sailing speed. Some days we were becalmed. There were days of cloudless sky without a breath of air, with viscous sea and blistering sun. The wheel would be lashed down with no man to attend it, the sailors all lolling in the sunshine on the fo'c's'le head. It was all so different from the times when gales were blowing and two men were on the wheel, fighting to keep control of it. On the quiet days I watched for hours, the shaft of sunlight striking fathoms deep into the clear blue water. Portuguese men-of-war sailed by leisurely trailing their drapery, pulsing their clear jellied bells in blue iridescence.

Bob Wakamea was with Sister and me so much of the time these days. He must have raced through his work so as to be at the rail so much with us. Men at sea were always interested in what was happening around them, and Father was very permissive when we girls were being entertained or instructed.

Bob would get a canvas bucket and start fishing for Portuguese men-of-war by maneuvering the bucket in the water to get under one of the creatures and gently lift it on board. Then he poured the water and the crystal being into a bucket on deck, cautioning, "Don't touch, whatever you do, just look. It's poisonous and painful." We spent hours watching while Bob ran back and forth, attending to his chores, and watching with us until the transparent bell with its trailing regalia was finally returned to the sea.

One such calm day I saw the wonder fish of my young life. It was a marvelous blue-green iridescence, about three feet long, and had a very blunt nose and was resting close beside the ship's side. It shimmered through the clear water in all its striking beauty. Bob appeared and looked, too. "Dolphin,"* he said and promptly left whatever he was doing to get hook, line, and bait. The instant he lowered the baited hook, the fish snapped at it and Bob had it out of the water and on deck.

Right before my disappointed eyes, the blue-green fish began to change color and fade and a fish like any other fish was finally before me. Fresh fish for all hands for dinner that night. A kind of celebration, too, for the "dolphin" was a delicacy more desired than the multitudes of blue bonito the sailors used to spear from the bow. The sailors had some way of standing on the heavy chains that went from below the jib boom to fasten onto the prow of the ship. When the weather was good for spearing, bonito was fresh for eating and it was good. There was plenty of bonito for frying,

* The fish dolphin as opposed to mammal dolphin.

baking, chowder, and fish cakes but the "dolphin" was par excellence.

After a lifetime of wondering and some tepid research when I thought of it, I met some seamen who instantly recognized my description of the "dolphin." No, they hadn't anything to do with dolphins as we usually thought of them, but, yes, sailors called them dolphins. Much later, in reading Hardy's *Great Waters** he mentions the "sailor's dolphin—blue-green, the most beautiful fish in the sea." Its true name, *Coryphaena*. A nagging, midget mystery of a lifetime was solved.

Another such day of limp sails, tied wheel, and smooth waters, Father called us to the rail of the poop deck. He had a large iron hook fastened to a long length of rather heavy line and was waiting for Bob to return from the galley with a ham bone. He was up to something interesting, but looking over the rail we saw only the usual shafts of sunlight going deep into the water. When Bob came back he gave the ham bone to Father and helped him attach it to the big hook.

Some of the sailors came to look. Everyone leaned over to watch Father lower the line gently into the water. No sooner had the hook and ham hit the water when from beneath the ship a long black shark slid swiftly past the hook, made a sudden turn, and with white belly up, took the hook and ham bone in one swift gulp. In a flash, the men watching on deck began to haul, holding tightly to the rope, but the shark's powerful struggle and thrashing were almost too much.

* Hardy, Sir Alister, *Great Waters,* Harper & Row, New York, 1967.

The men managed to work the shark, still in the water, along the side of the ship, on the outside of the rigging, to a place on the main deck where there was more room. More men came running to help with the hauling when they heard the excitement on that calm day. With concerted pulling the big shark was finally pulled over the side and on to the deck, thrashing frighteningly. We all stood well away from it, you can be sure. With a b'la'ne pin in hand, Father watched his chance and struck the shark on the snout. Then, while it lay stunned a minute, he ripped the length of the belly open with a knife from the galley, revealing the lovely white mother-of-pearl insides of the shark. Father explained, you could never be sure a shark was dead just because it was quiet, and sometimes sharks had young in them, but not that day.

Shimoda in white apron stood by quietly and at last asked if he might have the eyes. Permission granted, he removed them. Here was fresh fish for all hands for a month, but only Shimoda took any part of it. I asked Mother about this but all she could say was, "Perhaps the eyes are a delicacy in Japan." As for the rest of the shark, sailors feared and hated them so much they wouldn't even eat them when it meant fresh meat. The carcass of the shark was finally dumped over the rail to be food for his own kind.

There is a Chinese saying that one picture tells more than a thousand words. The whole day's lesson of the catch was inscribed in my mind like a painting. The long, dark form sliding out mysteriously with effortless motion from beneath the ship where nothing was in sight before, anywhere around us, the flash turn to gulp the bait—the lesson: don't ever fall overboard! Very sinister, the movements of a shark in deep water and very beautiful, easy, and graceful, not like any other fish.

Another motionless morning we got up to find the ship surrounded by huge, sleeping turtles. In every direction around us were the small, dark, unmoving islands on the sunny surface of the sea. After breakfast, Father had one of the boats quietly lowered into the water, had a rope ladder thrown over the side of the ship, and with two men along to row and help him, they set off very quietly. For the others on board, there were orders to plug the scuppers on the main deck between the forward and after hatches to fill the area with ocean water. Mother stayed in the cabin while all the excitement was going on, as she always did when Father got into a small boat at sea. My sister and I hung over the bulwarks and watched the quiet rowing of the men in the boat with Father in the prow. They moved farther and farther away from the ship. Letting the boat float softly up behind a turtle, Father grabbed a hind fin and flipped the turtle over on its back, then he and the two men with him picked it up and put it in the boat, still on its back, and rowed back to the ship with it. The turtle was hauled up and placed right side up in the shallow lake that had now been formed on the main deck. They made several trips until there were six or eight turtles in the area. All during the day the men added water so that the turtles could be alive and fresh for Shimoda to butcher as needed. While they lasted we had turtle steaks, which were fine, and turtle stew and soup, which was not so fine to us children, perhaps because of the heat of the day. The adults talked about the turtle food for a long time after.

On the South American trip I saw the scuppers plugged again, this time plugged for rain, along with all the washtubs and pails available. This was the only replacement of fresh water that was possible on the longer trips where saving of fresh water was mandatory, and used only for drinking and cooking, so that a lively downpour always brought the same response.

An incident of a single rainstorm at sea at night is vivid in my memory for all times. Father woke me from sleep, wrapped a blanket around me, and carried me up on deck. Sleepy little girl that I was, I saw only a quiet night of beautiful full moon, a night of shining water. Father pointed to starboard a way behind us and said, "Watch over there," pointing to the one dark spot on the sky. "It's rain and I think it will hit the ship." The section of darkness was moving toward us even though clear moonlight and stars and gentle sea were all about us. As I sleepily watched, the dark spot approached rapidly. Then Father drew me into the shelter of the companionway as the heavy rain slammed the ship with a bang, obliterated everything before us, crossed the ship, and as quickly passed beyond the lee side. Father took me out of the shelter of the companionway to see the moon shining on the waters, and the downpour that had hit the ship a moment before going its way across the sea. Then he took me down to the cabin and tucked me in, to go back to sleep.

Sometimes I'm sure my laconic father must have been bursting with the beauty and wonders of the sea on which he spent so much of his life. His only way of communicating the marvels of it was to share it with someone. This he did with Mother for years, and when I got old enough, I fell heir for a short time. I wonder if he knew I'd never forget.

As we moved south, Father daily "shot" the sun. He pored over his charts in the chartroom where he had put a dot at 10°N and 117°W, my birthplace, but the winds and currents carried us rather wide of the mark on this trip. Father explained as we were passing his mark, "Coming back we will try again." The sun and water and sky looked very much alike from one place to another, but missing the spot on the chart seemed to us like passing up the old homestead. But coming back to San Francisco, we were again becalmed and again drifted far afield before we caught the first breath of wind to carry us north and home. In the chartroom we looked at the marked dot of my birthplace and knew we would never reach it again.

On balmy evenings in the tropics, there were harmonica solos from the fo'c's'le head and accordion solos aft. We walked under warm southern skies or hung over the rail and watched the ship's wake, alive with the sparkle and fire of phosphorescent plankton in the black sea. We watched the masts of the ship roll gently against the night sky, full of stars, as thick as morning dew. The logline ripped through the water in a fine spray that sparkled as if with diamonds. There were early evenings, too, when we raced to the deck for the sunsets. Beginning softly, almost imperceptibly, they bloomed into unimaginable forms and colors that covered the whole western sky from horizon to the zenith. At first gradually, then suddenly, they darkly faded into twilight, and were no more. The celestial show changed nightly, and we never missed a single one.

One sunny noon on the way south, we crossed the Equator. Sailors knew this was coming and readied themselves for it. The old-timers—and one trip made anyone an old-timer—were getting ready for the initiation of the one or two tenderfeet among the crew. They made Neptune wigs and beards of short lengths of unravelled rope and short white draperies befitting the sea god. At the proper time and place—notified by Father, who approved of the high jinks—work stopped. All hands were on the main deck for the celebration. There was much horsing around which ended with buckets full of salt-water poured repeatedly over the heads of the initiated, who stood there and took it as had every sailor in the world before him, knowing that the rite, once over, made him a full-fledged, deep-water sailor by proclamation, and all lack of experience be damned.

There was more sailing to gentle winds and the quiet everyday routine of a ship at sea. Then one day Father announced we had passed Cape Blanco and would be in Antofagasta, Chile soon.

When the ship finally came to anchor in the bay, we learned that the consignees had failed during our long trip down, and Father had to find another buyer for the cargo. Our short stay in Antofagasta wasn't too pleasant in other ways. Antofagasta streets were dusty and unpaved, water was sold by the bucket from burro-back. Everything seemed dirty and dry. The bay was turbid and yellow and shark infested, the native steve-dores periodically took off their clothes to shake them over the side into the water to rid the garments of ver-min. Cats that strayed and crossed to the docks from the ships were caught and skinned on the dock, and the skins thrown into the water to float as a grisly reminder of hunger. For the first time, I saw the haws-ers that tied the ship to the docks equipped with metal shields to keep the rats from climbing aboard. In for-eign parts, rats were equated with bubonic plague.

Father finally arranged for a buyer for the cargo and we set sail northward again, but we were not through with Antofagasta just yet. An otherwise lovely day at sea was severely disrupted by a movement of Mother's firstborn—reaching to scratch her head! Mother watched for a minute and a minute was all it took to repeat the casual gesture. Mother grabbed my head, looked, and called Father. One look for him was enough for a diagnosis—lice, and the remedy was applications of kerosene! My Danish mother was ready for a strait-jacket, but first the lice had to be exterminated. After that was over, she didn't need it. A most unhappy child spent perhaps a week of daily applications of kerosene to her scalp. After that, there were consultations and examinations to be sure that nits and eggs had been thoroughly purged. Perhaps a layer of scalp went along with the purgings, but when it was through, I had the dubious distinction of being the only one on the ship to have been lousy! And after Mother had been so busy keeping us away from the Hindu longshoremen in Ladysmith (British Columbia). Was some Hindu god getting his revenge?

At Callao, we sailed inside the breakwater and dropped anchor in the opaquely yellow bay the same color as Antofagasta's, but here all similarity ended. Callao was alive with activity and hustle. The launches running back and forth to ships riding to anchor, the lighters loading and unloading in the bay, the officials boarding us to do whatever business was necessary with Father. Vendors in small boats brought us fresh fruits and vegetables. I had my first heavenly taste of small pink bananas; Father bought a whole stalk of them for us. There was some disagreement between Father and Mother over this but Father insisted we should eat the bananas because we liked them and they were good for us. Finally, Mother told us we could eat them in the cabin but not run around the deck eating bananas. I interpreted this to mean that the bananas were a special treat, like our afternoon tamales and eels and limburger cheese, and not for everyone. It made perfectly good sense.

The waterfront in Callao was all beautiful stonework, with stone stairs going into the water where our ship's boat landed to put us ashore. If I was impressed with Callao, it was nothing compared to the short trips we made inland to visit Lima on several occasions. I thought it was more modern, more beautiful than any city I had ever seen. There were plants and greenery in profusion, fascinating outdoor cafes, a beautiful park, a zoo such as I had never seen before. Beautiful beaches, beautiful streets, beautiful houses—so big, so fancy, so elegant—everywhere, it seemed, all the houses in Lima were like that. We visited the home of the new consignee and entered a room the size of a large hall, a couple of stories high, it seemed to me, with a glass dome above and black and white squares on the floor. Large plants were growing in pots around the room. I thought there were no hovels in Lima or poor people to go with them, only culture and manners and beauty and elegance. And church bells.

Before we left Lima, we had been to a bullfight in the big Lima arena. I think Mother did some muttering about this but her mutterings were lost in the color and excitement and noise of the extravaganza. After all, I thought, it was much better than the prize fights always being talked about on the ship and seen in the magazines that Father brought home, although we hadn't ever been to one; picadores and matadores were taking awful chances against the horns and feet and weight of the bulls. Not much difference between the two "sports" after all. Before we left Lima, Sister and I got rope-soled espadrilles to rest beside our kid and fur mucklucks from Nome and our beaded moccasins from the Sound. Mother came home with a beautiful diamond and ruby ring which she wore the rest of her life.

Father loved the sea, and for him the most beautiful places were the harbors of Rio and Sydney and San Francisco Bay. I loved the sea, too, and memories for me are rich forever, but Lima has always remained for me the city beautiful after that first and early exposure.

5

*"A Hot Time in the Old Town Tonight"**

SAN FRANCISCO was home port for *Snow & Burgess.*
Right across her black stern, white painted into deeply
chiseled cut-out letters were the words, *"Snow & Burgess—San Francisco"* for all the world to see wherever
she went. Sometimes I think that the large white letters were impressed into my memory the same way.
Other ships that Father sailed had names, too. The
beautiful four-masted barkentines, *Rolph* and *Hesperian,* and another five-masted schooner, *Rose Mahony,*
were all from San Francisco, too, but I can't remember
what the sterns of them looked like; mostly, I suppose,
because I had never looked up at them from drifting
boats, even though that was before I could read. The
other ships were Father's, and *Snow & Burgess* was
mine. I knew what those large, white letters said as
well as I knew the smell and feel and look of the wood-
planked wharves, the bay full of ferryboats and hay
scows, the tangle of masts along East Street (now the

---

* The title of a popular song written by Theodore Metz.

SAN FRANCISCO WAS BURNING . . . We had been out at sea during
the earthquake and fire of April 18, 1906, and we came in to the
last smoldering embers of the disaster. Nobody explained any of
this to the little girl watching from the deck. She was too little to
understand. From all over the burning area families fled with what
they could carry, to open spaces like this scene at Dolores Park in
the Mission. At first, tents were improvised, later the Army set up
rows of regular army tents. Thousands were homeless.

Embarcadero) and the sounds of San Francisco—the
"big city," city of cafes and theatres and big stores and
horse-drawn streetcars on the cobblestones. San Francisco was home to me—where all the relatives were,
where all the crews were signed on, where Pope &
Talbot's lumber yards were.

The excitement of coming into San Francisco began

with sighting Point Reyes light, Duxbury Reef, the Farallones, then the lighthouse on Mile Rock and the lightship. Then we sailed past the Potato Patch and Seal Rocks with the noisy barking seals, through the Golden Gate, and into the bay. Tom Crowley's Red Stack tugs were outside to meet us and follow us in, all the news of the last two months while we were at sea shouted through a megaphone; all the while there was the pestering of two small girls that we take a tow, which we seldom did. Father preferred to sail his big ship between the other ships anchored in the bay and the slow-moving ferries to drop anchor in his own spot beyond Meigg's Wharf or let the tugs berth us to Pope & Talbot's wharf at the last minute. The scuttling, puffing, whistling tugs were always an excitement for us, but Father's excitement was handling his big ship through bay traffic and he did it whenever possible. The last time, in my memory at least, that this happened was when I was going to college in Berkeley in 1922. A golden late-September afternoon he sailed the white-painted, four-masted barkentine *Rolph* into the bay amongst the ferry commuters going home for the day. The next morning when I arrived for class the whole campus was buzzing with the sight of the evening before. By that time, sailing ships were beginning to fade from the bay and the sight of a big one sailing in near sunset was a thrilling memory for all who saw it.

When I was on *Snow & Burgess* in the first decade of the century, the bay was still full of ships waiting to dock, and masts covered the waterfront of East Street.

Ships sailed from San Francisco carrying lumber and other cargoes to all the ports of the world: Hawaii, Japan, Australia, South America, around Cape Horn to the East Coast, to South Africa, to Europe. Father knew all the ships and was friendly with many of the captains. Names of ships like the *Samar, Inca, Pactolus, Sterling, Babcock,* and *Forester* were all a part of my childhood.

> *They mark our passage as a race of men,*
> *Earth will not see such ships as those agen*

says John Masefield, listing his own private catalog of "ships" in Liverpool and "the Mersey's windy ways."

Captain Watts of the *Pactolus* was picked by my sister at age five to marry after studying his picture in the *Master Mariners Journal.* I think the picture showed a youngish man sans whiskers or moustache, which made him seem younger. Anyway, the name *Pactolus* was intriguing and a further inducement toward matrimony. He certainly was her first love and the pronouncement left everyone a bit stunned. For me, I had no time for this sort of dalliance. I was committed in my loyalties to *Snow & Burgess* and its captain, so the rivalry and competition of any such ambivalence was not to be borne. I already knew the pain of this in another direction. The bark *John Ena* was bigger than *Snow & Burgess.* In addition, she was white-painted in contrast to the black-painted hull of *Snow & Burgess* and had such an array of canvas on her square-rigged masts as to strike a small heart with scalding

LOOKING SOUTH ON EAST STREET, THE VIEW FROM THE FERRY
BUILDING TOWER, BEFORE 1906 . . . East Street was where the
work of San Francisco's waterfront was done. If it was the sailors'
hangout, the ship captains were princes of the realm. And the captain of a smart sailing ship like the *Snow & Burgess* was a man to
be listened to. Needless to say we made the most of it, dressed in
our starchy best, with a dab of Mother's Florida water on us, as
we made the rounds with Father. The cigar store and saloon keepers along East Street were the most desirable people to know. After
handshakes they produced gum and candy and soft drinks on a
tray.

jealousy. *John Ena* not only looked like some huge,
beautiful yacht, but she also sported a figurehead
beneath her bowsprit which *Snow & Burgess* did not!
This was a serious omission that couldn't be discussed
with anyone. Fortunately we didn't see too much of

John Ena but when we did we talked and looked and talked and looked some more. She was an imposing sight—particularly with all sails set—and all ships suffered by comparison, including my own *Snow & Burgess*.

As soon as *Snow & Burgess* was tied to the dock, Father appeared in his shore clothes—white shirt with stiff white collar, dark tie, black suit. In winter, he wore a black Stetson hat, in summer, a Panama; the wearing of either seemed ordained solely by calendar date. And always his polished black shoes.

His first trip was uptown to the bank for money to pay off the crew. Every trip back to San Francisco, we could count on an argument between Father and Mother over these bank trips. Sensibly, she was worried about his carrying so much money around with him just as another might carry the family groceries. Father wouldn't have been caught dead with an armful of groceries or any other package, but carrying the payroll back to the ship he thought nothing of and scoffed at her concern. Mother read the papers and knew that men found floating in the bay among the piers had got there by carrying far less than Father did on these routine excursions. So, back in San Francisco every two months there was the argument. This time period could vary a bit but the argument didn't, and while I'm sure Father kept a good deal of money around the cabin as well, I never knew him to lock the doors when we were away.

When he returned to the ship from the bank, the big table in the dining room was spread with his account

THE CITY REBUILT BY 1910 ... Only the Ferry Building (built on pilings in 1896) survived the 1906 earthquake and fire. All the office buildings seen on this rainy afternoon were put up in the previous four years, and three new Market Street construction projects were still underway. A scatter of automobiles maneuver around horses and buggies and the numerous streetcars. It was a time when a motor car sold for just over $5,000 and a 2-bedroom cottage in Pacific Heights went for less.

books, the men were summoned to line up for payoff. Ledgers before him indicated the signing-on dates of the men with any withdrawals they had made while on the trip, a record of all slop chest purchases—clothing, tobacco, towels, and rain gear. Replacement of personal items was infrequent on the shorter trips but they could be vital to a seaman's functioning. Occasionally men started the trip with just what they were wearing. All items were totaled and deducted and signed for from the $30 a month seamen were paid. Father had the money laid out before him in stacks like gambler's chips—gold 20's, 10's, 5's, and 2½ dollars plus silver dollars, 50-cent pieces, quarters, dimes, and nickels. I'd never seen a penny in those early years.

After the fo'c's'le crew got paid came the regulars: cook, cabin boy, carpenter, mates—these last who mostly stayed with the ship for years. These people drew pay as they needed it and seemed to leave the rest with Father in the record book, like Shimoda who drew his balance periodically to go to Japan to visit his family.

After everything was stowed away and the men paid off, the ship settled into an unseemly quiet before unloading the cargo. The men went ashore and came back for their gear, some of them bringing candy for the little girls, chocolates in fancy boxes with ribbons on them in one-, two-, or even five-pound boxes for each. With so much candy around, we developed an early discrimination evidenced by the number of pieces with mouse-nibbled corners to test the flavor before rejecting. The sight of the box with the nibbled chocolates in them gave Father one of his "conniption" fits, as he called his frustration of not knowing how to handle the situation. Mother was always highly amused by this but wouldn't help him out, even if she knew what to do with a discipline problem in nothing flat. Father, protector of all women, confronted by his two small, soft, female counterparts, was like some giant Laocoön, minus son, of course, tangled in a frustration-serpent of his own temper but every bit as anguished and helpless as the statue I've looked and laughed at many times. When Father had moved his wordless conniption elsewhere, she would say, "Get rid of the stuff you don't want. You know your Father can't stand it around like that."

We gathered them up and put the pieces into the long tube of the toilet and into the bay they went. Will some anthropologist, 20,000 years hence, find the mounds preserved in bay mud, by then risen to some dry mountain peak, and wonder if this was food for the strange people who lived here?

Shimoda and Bob did much better with their gifts. When they returned they brought back small sacks of dried, crystalline melon and coconut, lichee nuts, and gum, all of which we attacked happily.

Father returned from shore trips with crayons and drawing books, clay pipes for making soap bubbles, rubber boots, and the very necessary small brooms. Sometimes he brought back bolts of material, never just a few yards, for Mother to make dresses of—China silk, dimity, dotted-Swiss, eyelet embroidery. Mother got magazines—*Red Book, Yellow Book, Munseys, Ladies*

Home Journal, Argosy, Leslies; books by Father's and Mother's favorite authors—Jack London (everything that came out!), Hall Caine, and Gelett Burgess. For the small fry, Hans Christian Andersen, the Brothers Grimm, *The Sleeping Beauty.* When Mother went ashore without us she returned with Jordan almonds, burnt peanuts, and small frying pans of marzipan "fried eggs."

Before Father went ashore, both in San Francisco and on the Sound, Mother's last words to Father were, "And don't forget scissors." As if he could! His small girls were addicted to putting Mother's large shears down the toilet bowl for the pleasure of hearing the heavy blades clank their way against the long tube of the toilet, into the water below. It was a hard habit to break!

Father was always dressed up in port, and when he took us with him on trips ashore, Sister and I were both dressed alike and to the teeth. One of us on each side of him holding his hands, dressed in our starched and ruffled best, black patent leather shoes with white kid tops, long white lisle stockings, wide-brimmed beaver hats in winter, Leghorns in summer with streamers going down our backs, thick white teddy bear coats in winter, tailored black-and-white checked in summer.

Dressed in our starchy best with a dab of Mother's Florida water on us, we made the rounds with Father. We visited the offices of Pope & Talbot and sat quietly while business was being transacted. Then we visited the ship chandler, Harry Haviside, where new white

THE CROWLEY BROTHERS MAKE A DEAL ... Tom and Dave Crowley were smart Irish businessmen. Their Red Stack tugboats were essential to bringing the big sailing ship safely to wharfside. Father preferred to sail his big ship between the other ships anchored in the bay and drop his anchor in his own spot beyond Meiggs Wharf, and let the tugs berth us at Pope & Talbot's pier later on. Knowing them as smart operators then, we might have guessed that one day the Crowley tugboat operation might have a monopoly on the bay, but the extent of Crowley's modern international business would have boggled our imaginations.

canvas sails were being made, scattered across a loft floor with men working on them. Haviside's office was on the lower floor with space around for horses and teams on which to load and unload the finished and unrepaired products, and there was plenty of addi-

tional space around them for parking horses and wagons as needed. This seemed to be the common practice
for those days. Mother's cousin Esther and her husband Nils had a dairy in the downtown area of 9th and
Clementina which was burned out in the 1906 fire and
earthquake; the dairy had this same arrangement. The
teams and wagons drove in from the street, loading
and unloading huge cans for the receiving and delivery
of milk. A business with transportation needs took care
of its own parking on its own property, as well as the
care and storage of horses and wagons.

The milk came from the rural area around Twin
Peaks where the grass grew green and cows wandered
loose, to feed and thrive. I think I would have seen or
heard of cows around 9th and Clementina if there had
been any; the area was on the outer edges of downtown San Francisco, but I have no recollection of cows.
Only the horses and wagons and straw were definitely
there with the flies flying about and a strong odor of
stables.

Esther and Nils were Danish so it went without saying that everything was immaculate. They had their
apartment over the stable. If that last is something to
give pause, project yourself past the year 2000 and
wonder what people's reaction will be to the polluted
air we breath from our cars, then think no more about
it. Further, if any flies got past the screen door there
was always fly paper about to trap the critters.

Pope & Talbot had stables on the wharf at Third
and Berry Streets. Mr. Callaghan, who cared for the
horses, always came out to greet Father and his two

small girls. Father shook hands with Mr. Callaghan and, at his bidding, we girls did, too. When you went with Father there was a lot of handshaking as people were greeting the Captain as he walked along East Street. Sometimes these greeters were not so clean and seemed "down and out" but Father never seemed to notice "status" and the same dignified courtesy was extended to them as to the business people we visited.

Father knew all the barbers along East Street; all their waiting customers sat reading the *Police Gazette*. My sister and I knew the *Police Gazette* on sight—its flamboyant pink pages—but never in our small lives got the chance to look at one! Father sometimes brought them to the ship for himself and Mother to see but somehow they always managed to disappear, leaving a lifelong curiosity unsated but not forgotten. In 1972, I ran into a reproduction of the book under the same name. I bought it and showed my sister, but we agreed the nagging sense of something missing was not to be appeased. I threw it out.

The cigar store and saloonkeepers along East Street were the most desirable people to know. After hand-shakes, they produced gum and candy and soft drinks on a tray from the saloon. For Father there was usually a small glass and much friendly talk.

East Street was a very friendly place in those days and Father and his girls were equal to the whole length of it. But sometimes Mother wasn't so friendly when we got back to the ship and she saw the gifts and smelled Father's breath fill the cabin; but then, she had missed all the fun.

APPLE SELLER ON EAST STREET . . . When we were growing up, prows of the sailing ships came right up to East Street—you can see the Ferry Building clock tower in the background. It was a wonderful noisy place; I knew the smell and feel and look of the wood-planked wharves and the tangle of masts along East Street. A figurehead like the handsome one in this view would have been a source of envy, as *Snow & Burgess* lacked that partiuclar maritime embellishment.

Our trips with Father paid off in many ways. He made arrangements (through proper channels, of course) for us to go on pony rides with Pope & Talbot's young delivery boy, Carl, who made trips all over town in a two-wheeled wicker cart, pony-drawn with open back and just enough room in the two front corners for Sister and me. Carl drove the dappled pony, clumping along the cobblestones and making the deliveries and pick-ups while we waited in the wagon. Around three o'clock, Carl would head for the hitching post in front of Haas's candy store on Market Street. Sometimes we went to Foster & Orears in the Ferry Building. Father always gave Carl money for a treat for us and it was here we had our first ice cream sodas. The wonder of them in so many new flavors has lasted a lifetime. When Father came back to the ship and announced that Carl had gone away to school and there would be no more pony and cart trips around San Francisco, it was a sad day for us. But the delivery service was giving way to more modern means of communication such as the telephone, which was coming into more common use about this time. When Sister and I left the ship for school in 1910, we had the only telephone on our block in Alameda so that Father could let us know when he got into port and when he would be home.

The memory of the dark-haired young Carl with his pony and cart and Haas's many-flavored ice cream sodas is as clear and keen now as then. Mr. Callaghan and the stables were still here, and we shook hands with him whenever we passed him to visit the ship.

Days in port were taken up with the hustle of unloading the cargo of lumber and logs. Swaying gaffs and booms, the whistle of donkey engines, cargo swaying overhead with tally men on the docks to count the pieces of lumber, and over all the noise, voices giving orders to longshoremen. Only on Sundays was there time for us to investigate the docks. Lumber piles made lovely playhouses on a Sunday morning. Smooth-stacked on top, sides, and front, the back end toward the bay stuck out in uneven, irregular lengths, giving an unglassed window view of the bay scene. By hunting a bit, we could find just the right place, properly furnished with a jutting bed of lumber for the dolls we remembered to bring along. It was a "house" with a waterfront view of the bay with its muddy waters and rainbow spills of oil that changed shape and color with the gently lapping waters. A hay scow was usually somewhere ahead tied up at the wharf bringing food for the many working horses of the day. The bay was full of hay scows on weekdays but on a quiet Sunday all the hustle ceased along the docks. At sea, when the deck was loaded, the same arrangement of lumber ran up to the dining room, making playhouses there, too, but someone was always walking over your house, spoiling the fantasy. And the ship was lower in the water when loaded and more apt to take on seas, making for wet housekeeping and wet paper doll children. But Sunday, after breakfast on the dock in the sunshine, amid the fresh smelling lumber, we found the right apartment for ourselves with jutting wood for beds and stoves and chairs and plenty of room to play in. Later Mother would call us to dress for going "uptown" or across the bay on the ferries.

Then one day a serpent was there in my sunny Eden. Looking up, I saw an exhibitionist before me, watching—motionless, exposed. I stared, frightened, then slowly reached for my doll and her blanket and fled back to the ship. I knew I had seen something I

SHIP *BEACON ROCK* LOADING SALMON AT HOWARD STREET WHARF, CA. 1907 . . . One of the most familiar waterfront sights and sounds were the huffing and puffing of the little steam-driven donkey engines. One such "stevedore's donkey" is seen here directly under the sling of wooden crates, and another appears on the opposite side, beyond the horse-drawn drays, where the *Bayonne* is loading cargo. These small but powerful steam engines gave the power needed to raise heavy packing crates—in this case, eighteen at a time—into the hatches. The man who ran them was called "a donkey man."

shouldn't have seen and never again visited the recesses of the lumber pile.

Sundays were our days for entertaining or visiting. Company came in the early afternoon and stayed into the late evening, food and drink aplenty. Saturday nights were reserved for our more private parties for close friends and relatives. Some of the friends and relatives belonged to the Danish singing society, Lyren, and made lovely music into the night. I don't remember ever leaving and going to bed, yet I would awaken

GETTING AROUND SAN FRANCISCO WAS ALWAYS FUN ... Here, the Sutter Street cable car makes its way past typical wooden rowhouses of San Francisco, with shops on the ground level and bay-windowed flats above. This was called a California-styled car because half of it was open to enjoy the air, admire the view, and hop off and on with aplomb. It was always with a sense of adventure that we got aboard the toylike, but dependable little cars to ride up to the top of one of San Francisco's big hills.

in my bunk in the morning, no doubt having passed out from sheer sleepiness, helped along by a small shot glass of diluted wine or some beer we were allowed to have with the guests, some of whom passed out before we did. Father had the reputation of being able to drink everyone "under the table," of never showing it when he was "three sheets in the wind" or "carrying a deck load." He was always on hand to take care of his guests. I don't know how the others got home but no one was about in the morning when we woke up. There was no phone on the ship or anywhere near it to call a horse cab. Perhaps someone walked up to the 3rd and Townsend depot* for one. No one seemed to think anything of walking distances and waiting for the horse-drawn cars that were few and leisurely that time of night.

Horsecabs were wonderful. They could be driven on either side of the street in all directions up to the hitching posts in front of stores, restaurants, and the-atres, where a weight was dropped to keep the horses from wandering away. No drunk-driving nonsense there, the horses had more sense than to drink with the passengers they hauled. Everyone had time in those horse-and-buggy days to go in leisure. Even the occa-sional auto couldn't go much faster than a horse.

Father loved to pile us all in a horse cart, and there were drives through Golden Gate Park on Sunday, drives to the Cliff House for dinner, to Sutro Baths, and the strange sights of the museum, drive back to the ship at night after an evening on the town. Mem-ories of pale skies with dawn just breaking, of horses' hooves against the cobble-stoned streets, finally clomping hollowly on the wooden planks of the wharf after an all-night dance where Sister and I danced together at ballroom's edge or Father took us, one at a time, for a trip around the room with the grown-ups. Then, after the dance, we would go with the crowd to the Hof Brau or Portola Louvre for dancing while the kitchen prepared oyster loaf for all.

Sometimes Father and Mother stepped off to parties

* Presently at 4th and Townsend.

THE FAMILIAR SIGHT OF THE CLIFF HOUSE . . . A storybook castle on a rock, one of the last sights to wave goodbye to as *Snow & Burgess* passed through the Golden Gate, heading out to sea. Built in 1895, the ornate wooden structure burned on September 7, 1907. Its concrete replacement was never as grand, but there remained an enchantment about this farthest point of land, near Seal Rock. It was our best place to greet Father's incoming ship, as the flag dipped in formal salute to us, waiting there, hanging over the railing, and waving like crazy ones.

without us, telling us Shimoda or Carpie was spending the night in the cabin because he had painted his room. No question here because all sailors knew, even very small ones, that you couldn't sleep in a freshly painted room because of the fumes the paints had in those days. Carpie and Shimoda painted their rooms a lot in San Francisco, but there were still many nights that we took in the bright lights of the city, especially the theatres.

San Francisco was a big show-town then and had

been since the Gold Rush days. We went regularly to the Pantages on Market Street and the Orpheum on O'Farrell Street, where Father always had a box for us with an unobstructed view of the show and room to wiggle and whisper without bothering anyone. Mostly, though, we were too fascinated to stir. We loved Kolb and Dill, the German comedians, and Weber and Fields, the Jewish comedians, and much later I married the blond son of a black-faced comedian with the Billy Emerson minstrels. (My father-in-law was born in San Francisco in 1859 when the skyscraper metropolis by the Golden Gate was not much more than a tent city.) Father loved "Casey at the Bat" though I never knew him to go to a ballgame, Harry Lauder with the kilt and gnarled cane singing "I Love a Lassie" and "Roamin' in the Gloamin'" in his marvelous burr. Once we went to the Cort Theatre to hear Chauncy Alcott sing in his lush Irish tenor "When Irish Eyes are Smiling" and "My Wild Irish Rose," closing the show by singing before the curtain until the last, lingering loiterer was finally out of the theatre. I'd never heard such a voice before—rich, full, rollicking, easy-flowing. But for Father the greatest music was the rousing band of John Philip Sousa and the greatest show on earth was the magic of Houdini.

Mother loved opera and went often before her marriage. Opera was one of the strong bonds between her and her cousin, Esther, besides the fact that they had grown up together in Denmark. Esther had a more-than-passable coloratura, studied singing, and sang arias from *Trovatore, Traviata, Rigoletto,* and *Carmen.*

SUNDAY PROMENADE IN GOLDEN GATE PARK . . . Father loved to pile us all into a horse cart and take us for a drive through Golden Gate Park. Everybody in San Francisco seemed to turn out in their fine rigs with high-stepping horses, moving at a smart clip. The park had band concerts, with my father's favorite rousing tunes by Sousa and visiting opera singers who delighted my mother. There was a fancy glass conservatory that had been imported from England and filled with rare flower displays and a giant lily pond; a big merry-go-round with mechanical music that included "Over the Rolling Waves We Go," and a museum with exotic Egyptian statues and a Pioneer Room.

Between them there was much told of Tetrazzini and Schumann-Heink and Caruso and Melba and Patti; of performances at the Morosco and Tivoli Opera House, of "Ben Hur" with real horses and chariots racing on a revolving stage, performances of Sarah Bernhardt and Nance O'Neil of Oakland, Blanche Bates, Mrs. Leslie Carter in "Du Barry," Ashton Stevens, Maude Adams in "Peter Pan."

We went to our first nickelodeon in San Francisco.

It was one afternoon when we were returning to the ship from a day of shopping with Mother and Esther, a day at Praeger's and Hale's bargains, at the Emporium and White House and City of Paris to catch up on the latest styles. I think it was an accident that we happened to be passing one of the just-coming-in moving picture houses. I know we stood some time on the sidewalk while Mother and Esther debated the burning issue of entering what I later learned to be a low-class form of entertainment—pictures that moved. When Mother and Esther got the matter settled, they came over to us and Mother—shaking her finger for emphasis and punctuation in our small faces—said we were going into the nickelodeon but we were not to tell anybody we had ever been in, not Father, *not anybody* (which probably meant Esther's husband, Nils). We promised.

We entered a small, dark, level room about the size of a mom-and-pop grocery store or a saloon on East Street, all very dark with loose seats or benches strung across in front of the screen. In black-and-white, in rapid, jerky motions, the movements of two boxers, moving in fast, socking each other, knocking each other to the floor, jerking back on their feet. A couple of rounds of this and Mother and Esther had had enough. They had seen that pictures could move. We small ones had only been bored. What was all the fuss about? We had seen better fights on board ship than the jerking, around-up-down, lunge-sock, miss, rapid-fire movements of the two boxers. Sometimes grownups didn't make sense. Father boxed every morning with his punching bag—though not in trunks—making rhythmic clip-clip sounds against the bedroom ceiling while we listened. When there was company, one of the major topics of conversation was the championship prize fights that had either passed or were coming up—Jim Jeffries, Jack Johnson, Gentleman Jim Corbett, Jesse Willard, and all the scuttlebutt that surrounded each, particularly Jack Johnson. He was the first black fighter ever to become world's champion, which was considered sensational, not only in itself but also because of all the white women who "threw" themselves at him. We accepted all this as true because another cousin of Mother's was married to a fight promoter, and being in the game, he knew. Father didn't have too much to say about this but Mother was "scandalized" for quite some time, in spite of Lazarus and Mrs. Lazarus—he of the gentle, tender manner and melodious Jamaican speech, and she, the cockney, ready to weep and taking umbrage at every glance. Mother had almost been ready to do battle in her defense, but this was different. Truly, grownups didn't make much sense sometimes.

Other conversations with guests that made for "scandalized" cluckings were the Stanford White shooting by Harry K. Thaw and the doings of the notorious Evelyn Nesbitt; the activities of the suffragettes and the Bloomer Girls who wore pants (if you could call them pants!) and rode bicycles with their ankles showing; Donaldina Cameron, who saved thousands of "sing-song" girls from the slave dens of Chinatown, the Mayor Schmitz-Abe Ruef scandal that rocked City Hall for years; French artistes and absinthe;

Elinor Glyn's shocking novel, *Three Weeks,* which Mother read, of course.

For Father, the Polar expeditions of Amundsen, Cook, Scott, and Perry were equivalent to today's space travel and moon landings! How he would have loved and marveled at these last! Once when we were in Puget Sound, he got us up in the middle of the night to go up on a hill to see Halley's comet since we might not ever see it again in our lifetime.

Another big, recurring mystery and topic of conversation was the disappearance of Captain Joshua Slocum, world-famous American sailor, who, after sailing around the world alone in his 36-foot *Spray,* disappeared without a trace into the oblivion of the Bermuda Triangle.

One day, a lone visitor to the ship talked so quietly to Father's courteous questions that we small fry left to seek the sunshine on deck for a more interesting scene. When the guest left, Father walked him to the gangway and they were still talking. For days after, Father kept shaking his head to Mother: such a nice man, so intelligent, so well-mannered. But a Socialist? And he'd shake his head again. What was a Socialist? And why was he the only one who fit this label to visit us? I knew Father wasn't one to be thrown by other people's ideas but this kept bothering him for all of a couple of days—good Bull Moose Republican, Teddy Rooseveltter, that he was.

Another visitor to the ship left an indelible impression on my childhood, if a symphony of soft, gray chiffon and matching gray boa of ostrich feathers could be

FOUR-MASTED, WHITE-PAINTED *HESPERIAN* . . . Built in Humboldt
County, California 1918, Father took her over when *Snow & Burgess* was sold. She belonged to shipping magnate "Sunny Jim"
Rolph, San Francisco's most popular mayor. On the strength of his
ebullient charm and dapper good looks, and in spite of his careless
attitudes toward professional ethics, he managed to hold that office
for nineteen years, and later was elected governor. *Hesperian* measured 1395 tons and was 231.4 feet by 45.5 feet by 18.6 feet. She
made it to New Zealand on her maiden voyage in an unheard of
56 days.

called indelible. This was another of Mother's cousins,
Annie, graduate of Miss Snell's Seminary for young
ladies in Oakland, classmate of Nance O'Neil, the popular actress, and married to the fight promoter already
mentioned. She and her husband toured the country
and were rarely seen in San Francisco, but once when
she was here she came to the ship. Once seen she was
never forgotten. She was another composite creature
straight from the pages of the theatre magazines Father

brought back to the ship. Here were my favorites, Billie Burke of the long braids, Anna Held, Lillie Langtry of the low-necked gowns and voluptuous bosoms, visiting the ship! Huge hat with ostrich plumes, the scent of violets buried in gray chiffon shoulder, elegant draperies disdainfully sweeping the decks as she walked; nobody ever—in the flesh—looked like this again. For myself, before I'd gotten around to this kind of elegance it was gone and the "flapper" girl was in. I did make the wrapped-around-head braids, but the voluptuous bosom was definitely out and stylish bosoms were flat as young boys'. It was "in" and I was "in," to Father's horror, I'm sure, though he never said as much.

Mother was in high-necked, long-sleeved, tailored shirtwaists with an incredibly small, tightly laced waist. Even her seal coats were close-fitting and trim. All the other women wore pretty much the same type of clothes. They wore hats for every casual outing with stuffed birds nesting on them.

My young life was colored with tales of Andy Furuseth and the sailors union—wild tales of bodies being found in the bay, robbed of their pay, boardinghouse keepers on the waterfront who doped and shanghaied sailors for offshore jobs at so much a head; the aforementioned Eugene Schmitz scandal that rocked City Hall for all the years of my seafaring days; the panic of Cleveland's administration and the hard times that followed; the shooting of McKinley; the thrilling events of Father's hero, Teddy Roosevelt, and the Rough Riders of San Juan Hill in the Spanish-American War. All remembered as if yesterday. No radio, no tele-

vision—only the many daily papers to keep us belat-
edly informed. The small, growing city supported five
papers! The *Examiner, Chronicle, Call, Bulletin, Daily
News*—the last pro-labor and therefore radical.

Between the flow of company to the ship, there were
trips to Marin County by ferryboat and the open train
ride on the crookedest railroad in the world that wound
its way up Mt. Tamalpais, there for lunch or dinner in
the fog or sunshine. There were trips in other ferries
across the bay and more trains to visit relatives in Alameda, to Idora Park and Shell Mound Park in Oakland, Dania's picnic grounds; trips to Hayward through
lupine- and poppy-covered hills and down the penin-
sula of San Mateo in spring through blossoming apri-
cot orchards, smelling heavenly, on to dirt roads where
we'd be the only car sometimes—a tin lizzie—and had
at least one flat or engine trouble each trip, which never
seemed to bother anyone. Cars were few and far between
and you expected to have trouble or you'd have hired
a horse! Breakdowns seemed part of the fun of riding
an automobile. No such thing as service stations or
garages anywhere about, so while we waited for someone to help or get help, we roamed the fields picking
lupines or poppies—the blue and gold of California—
that spread over the acres of free hills about us.

There were Master Mariners excursions around the
bay on *Snow & Burgess,* with tons of food and drink
set up on tables about the decks, and crowds of members having a good time to music. The youngsters were
slightly bored, we'd seen so much more sailing at other
times for real that this sailing around the bay seemed

as nothing until a small emergency occurred. As is the way of kids, I had to go and right now! I made for the bathroom. It was crowded with women. Now, the bathroom with separate toilet was twice the size of my present one—perhaps more. The bathroom itself contained a washbasin with drawers on both sides for towels and washcloths and a large, covered bathtub, a large medicine-liquor closet opposite with plenty of space to move around in. There must have been a dozen women milling around.

I went for Mother. All I got was: with all these people on board I would simply have to wait my turn. Anyway, why did I always have to wait until the last minute—as if a kid ever did anything else! I took my misery back to the bathroom with resentment and indignation, to wait. My ship, my bathroom, and I couldn't even go to the toilet! Mother was right. Without having to open her mouth, or me, mine, one of the women took in the twitching situation at a glance, got the small girl into the toilet at the first opening, and saved the day for me.

One memory of early San Francisco that has stayed with me for years was coming into the bay and casting anchor. It was a sunny day, but the sun shone through heavy haze. Somehow San Francisco wasn't recognizable to the small girl surveying it. There were no wharfs, no buildings, no friendly tugs. Only the sun filtered through the heavy smoke. We had been out to sea when the earthquake and fire of April 18, 1906, had leveled San Francisco, and we came in to the last smoldering embers of the disaster. Nobody explained any of this

SUTRO GARDENS OVERLOOKED THE ENTRANCE TO THE GOLDEN GATE . . . Adolph Sutro built his gardens on a high bluff above his Cliff House and Sutro Baths, whose golden domes reflect his taste for opulence. For seafaring families like ours, this became the ideal place to watch ships make their way past Point Bonita Lighthouse in the Marin headlands, on their way through the narrow strait of the Golden Gate. The vessels in this view have passed the dangerous "potato patch," but tides at the gate were always swift encounters.

to the little girl watching from the deck. She was too little to understand, anyway, but the memory of what she had seen that day stayed with her for many years until she read of the disaster and learned that we had come in after it was almost over.

Came the day of taking leave of San Francisco. There were so many days of taking leave in my young life that the memory is as clear as yesterday. They began with being towed from the dock by bustling tugs, pulling, nudging, guiding. Our own donkey engine was snorting in preparation of raising sails, orders were shouted and repeated from one end of the ship to the other, sailors were running back and forth. We moved slowly past the wharves, and before we reached the Golden Gate all sails were set and flapping. As we did so many times, we waved good-bye to the Cliff House and Seal Rock, and once beyond the Gate, depending on the winds, the tugs dropped hawser to sail around the stern to wish us a good trip, see you soon, and farewell. We were on our own with the sea and sails and wind, all settled down to sea-life for the next two weeks.

Later, when we girls moved ashore to go to school, we frequently went out to the Cliff House to watch Father go to sea. The first few years we didn't go. Father was still on the San Francisco-Puget Sound run and home rather frequently. As 1914 approached, he was making the long trip to Australia, sometimes gone for as long as 14 months, so that seeing him off became something of an event. Sometimes we went to the Cliff House with Mother, sometimes with a friend while Mother went out with the ship and came back with the tug. This depended on the weather.

We went out to the Cliff House, at these times, by streetcar. I think the "Cliff Railway" had been destroyed by then, though we'd made many trips out by then on that, too. We usually got to the Cliff House before *Snow & Burgess* did, watched the seals on Seal Rock with their insistent barking, and climbed all around, but always keeping one eye out for the ship and her tug because when the ship got opposite the Cliff House, the flag was dipped in formal salute to the girls waiting there, hanging over the railing, waving like crazy ones, while Father watched from the ship with his handy binoculars. When the ship was clear of the Gate and the hawser dropped, the tug came alongside for Mother. *Snow & Burgess* was off on another trip and we would watch awhile and then go into the Cliff House for lunch.

The last time we did this was on Saturday, July 22, 1916. It was a calm, slightly sunny day and Mother had gone out along with the ship. As usual, there was no provision to meet since Mother would disembark from the tug on one of the wharves and we'd come by streetcar from the Cliff House. We'd not meet until we got home in Alameda. Anyway, we knew there was to be a Preparedness Day Parade on Market Street with crowds of people out and no telling what kind of traffic- and people-tangles. A pleasant day so we dawdled, then finally started home by streetcar.

The parade seemed to be over when we got downtown, but somewhere on Market Street we were put off the streetcar and told we'd have to walk to the Ferry Building. We made our way through the crowds of people and police running all over and finally to the ferry and home. Mother was frantic when we got there. She told us someone had bombed the Preparedness Day Parade. She'd figured we could have been there around the time it happened. With no radio to give us instant coverage, all we could do was wait for the papers, which didn't give much but scare headlines.

Later we learned that Tom Mooney and Warren

Billings had been accused and arrested. Their trial went on for years. Eventually given the death sentence, commuted to life imprisonment by President Woodrow Wilson, they stayed in prison until 1939—23 years later!—until given a full pardon by California's Governor Olsen. By that time practically everyone conceded they had been subject to one of the most notorious railroadings in the history of law. The case was world-famous and never a day out of the papers from the beginning. But on that July Saturday in 1916, Mother decided that San Francisco was definitely changing—like Baudelaire's "Old Paris"*—and the girls were better off spending the rest of their growing years in quiet Alameda, where there was bicycling and tennis and swimming and picnics on the warm streets and parks and beaches.

But San Francisco for me, no matter how much she changes, will always be remembered as "The City by the Sea."

> *At the end of our streets is sunrise,*
> *At the end of our streets are spars;*
> *At the end of our streets is sunset;*
> *At the end of our streets—the stars.*

> —George Sterling

---

* Old Paris is no more. A town, alas, changes more quickly than man's heart may change."

EPILOGUE

My Father's Death

My father died September 26, 1938. He had taken a Depression job as ship's watchman, and my mother, husband, daughter, and I had driven him over to the *Barbara C.* right after dinner. We didn't go with him onto the ship, which was tied up on the Oakland Estuary. For awhile we loitered around the dock in the late sunshine. Then we waved to him and left, as he was talking to a man on the ship's deck.

The next day, mid-morning, my brother-in-law called me. This was unusual in itself. Even more so was his unaccustomed stumbling speech. Finally he got the words out to tell me what no one else had been able to: the body of my father had been found floating in the Alameda Estuary near the *Barbara C.* that morning. Coroner's deputies said the death was evidently due to drowning. An autopsy would be done.

The next few days were busy with funeral arrangements, then the funeral, then the autopsy. The report showed him to have been in good health, no abnormalities, no water in the lungs, but he did have a nasty cut on his forehead running up into the hair. In some unexplained manner, there being no witnesses, Father had evidently lost his footing, struck his head losing consciousness, fallen, and died in the water.

Mother didn't seem able to get over Father's death. Even after a year she still seemed shocked, different. For one thing, her sureness, the independence, was gone. There was a kind of resignation, a giving-up about her. One afternoon she and I were alone together. For the first time, Mother began to speak of Father's death.

"Do you remember the last evening we saw him?"

I did.

"Do you remember the man he was talking to on the ship?"

I remembered the man.

"That man was the mate of the *Rolph* that your father stood trial for. Father let the mate go in Chile because of the mate's brutal treatment of the sailors, who brought charges. The mate came to the house many times asking for your father, always with foul language and threatening to get him someday. I'm sure he killed your father that day."

It was my turn to be shocked.

"Surely you've told someone about this?"

"No," she said. "What good would it have done? It wouldn't bring him back. I couldn't stand to have all that hell-ship business dragged out and aired again. You know, that man blamed your father for the prison term of five years he served at McNeil Island, although it was the second term for a similar offense."

"But Father was legally cleared of all that. Even the *Seaman's Journal* accepted this."

She got up and walked to her desk, opened a small drawer and removed a pair of pink satin and kid baby shoes with matching stockings. She brought them over to me.

"You take these now," she said. "In all the years since your birth, he never went to sea without them."

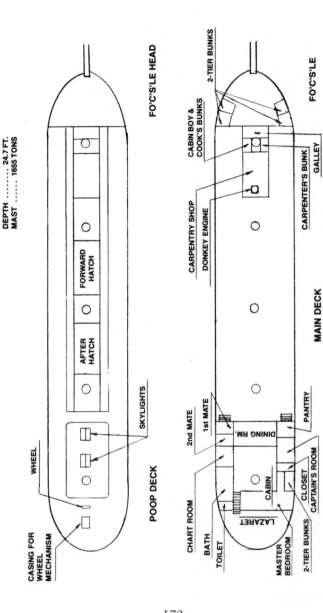

LENGTH ...... 228.5 FT.
BREADTH ...... 41.5 FT.
DEPTH ...... 24.7 FT.
MAST ...... 1655 TONS

FO'C'S'LE HEAD

WHEEL

SKYLIGHTS

FORWARD HATCH

AFTER HATCH

CASING FOR
WHEEL
MECHANISM

POOP DECK

2-TIER BUNKS

CABIN BOY &
COOK'S BUNKS

CARPENTRY SHOP

DONKEY ENGINE

FO'C'S'LE

CARPENTER'S BUNK

GALLEY

MAIN DECK

LESTER ANDERSON

PANTRY

2nd MATE

1st MATE

DINING RM.

CHART ROOM

BATH

TOILET

CABIN

CLOSET

CAPTAIN'S ROOM

LAZARET

MASTER
BEDROOM

2-TIER BUNKS

SCHOONER SNOW & BURGESS

1878 - 1922

172

Appendix I

Being the Anatomy of a Big Ship from the Memory of a Small Girl*

WE generally entered the cabin on *Snow & Burgess* through the sky-lighted dining room. The dining room was large and bright and had a heavy table and benches that were riveted to the floor, so that nothing short of destruction of the whole room could have moved them.

There were several doors in the dining room. One led to the pantry, which was full of wooden racks that held the heavy ship dishes in high but unshifting stacks. In the pantry there was also a large space for setting the meals that were on their way from the galley to the dining room. The coffee was always boiling in the pantry, kept hot for the mates and captain, day and night, and it was there also that the frequent between-meal snacks were eaten.

Another door in the dining room opened into Father's stateroom. That room had a bunk with drawers beneath and also a clothes closet. There were also doors from the dining room that opened into the first mate's and

* See diagram titled *Schooner Snow & Burgess.*

second mate's rooms. The first mate's room was fairly large and had a desk, a bunk with drawers beneath, and a closet. The second mate's room was similar but somewhat smaller and had two bunks. All of the rooms were well-lighted during the day by portholes. At night, coal oil lamps provided light.

All the doors had heavy brass hooks that could be attached to brass eyes screwed into the walls, so that the doors could be fastened open and not bang with the movement of the ship. Still another one of these doors from the dining room opened into the cabin, which was spacious and was paneled with bird's-eye maple. A gilded, carved frieze ran around the top of the room. There were settees on either side of the cabin, and both of them were heaped with pillows made of suede and velvet. A large stuffed chair under the skylight was used by Mother when she read or sewed. The floor was covered by a rose-patterned Axminister carpet.

During the process of converting *Snow & Burgess* from a three-masted square-rigger to a five-masted schooner, a mast was placed right in the middle of the cabin. It spoiled the symmetry of the room and broke up the floor space, much to Mother's horror. That anyone could do such a thing to an otherwise large and lovely room was quite beyond her.

Mother's bedroom, which was located to one side of the cabin, had a big double bed and a built-in vanity dresser with large mirrors and drawers. There was also the neatly varnished slop chest from which the crew was supplied with clothes and sundries while the ship was at sea. Sister's and my bunks were also in the room against a good-sized clothes closet.

The companionway steps that led to the poop deck were adjacent to Mother's room. The small hallway leading to the steps had two doors, one to Mother's room and one to the bathroom. It was through these two doors that Father came when he brought us our morning "tonic." The solid, heavy door at the top of the companionway steps was kept open whenever the weather permitted.

The bathroom was very large, large enough to use as a dressing area, although we did not use it for that purpose. The toilet was within the bathroom but was in an enclosed space of its own. The toilet and washbasin were both fitted with wood covers that could be used as tables and benches when the toilet and basin were not being used. Around the washbasin there were plenty of shelves for towels and washcloths.

The bathtub was also enclosed in wood and had a cover that was lifted when the tub was to be used. The tub was big enough to hold both Sister and me during our weekly baths. When the tub was not in use, a kerosene stove sat on the wood cover. The stove was used for making coffee or heating tamales or hot water for beef tea in the mid-afternoon. Father's medicine chest and liquor cabinet were also in the bathroom.

The chartroom was directly opposite Father's room. It was a compact place, just big enough for a large, high table that held the rolled, blue-backed charts that Father used for daily markings. The table also acted as a desk and held the needle-sharp pencils beside the whetstone used to sharpen the pencils. Father would lay the point of the pencil flat against the palm of his hand and then, using the blade of the knife, cut along the side of the pencil point in the direction of his palm, until he achieved the finest point he could. With his pencils and the double-slate rulers joined by strips of shiny brass, he used to skim across the surface of the white-faced charts to show in his neat, precise lettering the day's knots from noon to noon.

To the left of the table was a high cabinet with shelves and low, carved wood railings. Charts not in current use were stored there. To the right of the table was another cabinet, built to the ceiling and used for Father's books—*American Practical Navigator, Ainsley's Examiner in Seamanship, McNevin's Practical Navigator,* and *Davis' Sun's True Bearing or Azimuth Tables 30°N to 30°S.**

One book that was often used was *Hill's Manual of Social and Business Forms,* which had advice for every occasion (e.g., "Etiquette at Home," "Gentility in the Parlor," "Conduct at Places of Public Amusement," etc.), as well as examples of business forms and other useful information.† Another handy volume was

---

* Bowditch, Nathaniel, LL.D., *American Practical Navigator,* United States Hydrographic Office, Washington, D.C., issued periodically. Thomas E. Ainsley, *Ainsley's Examiner in Seamanship,* Thomas E. Ainsley, South Shields, England, issued periodically, from late 19th century onward. Capt. E. McNevin, *A Guide to Practical Navigation,* A. L. Bancroft & Co., Printers, San Francisco, 1878 and subsequent editions. Capt. John E. Davis (R.N., F.R.G.S.) and Percy L. H. Davis (F.R.A.S.), *Davis' Sun's True Bearing or Azimuth Tables 30°N to 30°S,* J. D. Pitter, Edinburgh, 1913.
† Thomas E. Hill, *Hill's Manual of Social and Business Forms, A Guide to Correct Writing,* Hill Standard Book Company, Chicago, Illinois, 1890.

Scammel's *Cyclopedia of Valuable Receipts,* which supplied data on cooking, care of the skin, the judging and buying of horses, the mixing of cement, cures for various diseases, weather indicators, bicycle maintenance, and other topics.**

In boxes beside the books, Father kept his sextants, and in an adjacent drawer he kept his ledger records and his log book. The cabinets were made of the same bird's-eye maple as the walls of the cabin. No pictures were ever hung on the walls to mar the woodwork.

** Henry B. Scammel, *Cyclopedia of Valuable Receipts: A Treasure-House of Useful Knowledge, for the Every Day Wants of Life,* The Whitaker & Ray Company, San Francisco, California, 1897.

Appendix II

Being a Partial List of Ships That My Father,
Captain A. H. Sorensen, Sailed Out of
*San Francisco**

Reaper

Reaper was a three-masted "down-easter" built in
Bath, Maine in 1876. She was 211:6 by 39:2 by
24 feet and registered 1469 tons. In 1876 *Reaper*
was sold to Captain A. P. Lorentzen of San Francisco. Father was her master from the mid 1890s
until 1901, when *Snow & Burgess* was converted
to a five-masted schooner. *Reaper* burned in Port
Ludlow, Washington in 1906.

Snow & Burgess

Starting out as a full-rigged, three-masted "down-
easter," *Snow & Burgess* was built in Thomaston,
Maine in 1878. She as 228:5 by 41:5 by 24:7 feet
and had a gross tonnage of 1655:49. In 1900 she
was sold to Captain A. P. Lorentzen and con-

---

* When Father became a citizen of the United States he changed his name
from Anton Holmgaard Sorensen to Albert Henry Sorensen.

verted to a bark rig. Either my father or Captain Lorentzen decided to have her converted from a three-masted bark to a five-masted schooner, and the conversion was completed by 1901, when Father became her master. He stayed with her after she was purchased by Police Commissioner Andrew F. Mahony in 1916 for $35,000. In 1918, after World War I had begun, Mahony sold the 40-year-old ship, which was beginning to show wear, for $225,000. *Snow & Burgess* was sold for scrap in Portland, Oregon in 1921 for $3,000. In 1922 she was run up on the beach and burned.

Hesperian

Father became master of *Hesperian* in 1918, at the time that Mahony sold *Snow & Burgess*. The four-masted, white-painted barkentine *Hesperian* had just been built in Humboldt County, California for James Rolph, who was then mayor of San Francisco and who would later be governor of California. The ship weighed 1395 tons and her dimensions were 231:4 by 45:5 by 18:6 feet. One of four sister ships, she sailed her maiden voyage to New Zealand in 56 days. She was laid up in Antioch, California in 1924.

Rolph

Rolph was one of *Hesperian*'s sister ships and was completed in Humboldt County in 1919. Loaded with grain, she set sail for England under my father's command. In October or November of 1919, while anchored in the Thames River during a foggy night, the *Rolph* was rammed by a Belgian tramp steamer. Post-war shortages of manpower and materials delayed the repairs. In England, when Father learned the extent of the damages, he sent for Mother, Sister, and me. We all stayed on the ship while it underwent repairs in Liverpool and then came home to California through the Panama Canal at the end of September 1920. Actually, Mother, Sister, and I disembarked at Puget Sound and returned to San Francisco by train in order to return to school, while Father took the *Rolph* to her next port.

Father stayed with the ship for the next few years. In 1921, while in Australia, it was necessary to hire a new mate, and the only one available was Frederic Hansen. Hansen was called a tyrant by the crew, who narrated his cruelties in affidavits furnished by the United States consul at Antofagasta, Chile to the United States Attorney General. While the affidavits were being drawn up, Father paid off the mate, which made it possible for Hansen to escape from Antofagasta to England, in an attempt to flee prosecution for assault on the high seas.

The Wednesday, June 15, 1921 issue of *The Seamen's Journal,* the maritime union paper, had a detailed account of the sailors' charges against Hansen. On Wednesday, June 22, 1921, the same paper had an editorial that said, in part, "While the brutal indignities to which the crew of the barkentine *Rolph* were subjected are regrettable, it is hard for us to feel a maximum of sympathy for the victims. It is almost beyond belief in these days of enlightenment that a body of men can be found that would tamely submit to the aggressions of such brutes as the Mate Hansen." An old clipping in my possession dated August 3, 1921, in my father's handwriting, is of a *San Francisco Chronicle* article that is headlined, "Sea Captain to Be Tried for Cruelty." My father was to stand trial for his responsibility in the affair. Before Father's trial began, however, Hansen was captured, tried, and sent to McNeil Island, Washington for five years. Hansen had previously spent a year at McNeil Island in 1916, after being charged with murder but pleading guilty to the lesser charge of assault with a dangerous weapon. Hansen was reported to have speared rats with a sail needle on a stick to watch them wiggle. Father was subsequently acquitted of all charges against him, but while the affair lasted there was the sensational and unsavory talk of "the hell ship."

Rose Mahony

From the *Rolph* Father went to the *Rose Mahony*. She was a five-masted wooden schooner, with a square yard on the foremast. She was 2051 tons and measured 261 by 48:3 by 22:4 feet. The schooner was built in Benicia, California by Andy

Mahony and named for his wife. Father became master of *Rose Mahony* in 1924, and in 1925 he sailed her through the Panama Canal to Miami, Florida. The insurance on the ship expired halfway through the canal and it was not renewed, because she was so close to her destination. A freak typhoon off the Florida coast lifted the *Rose Mahony* onto the Miami waterfront and left her stranded there as the water receded. She remained there for two years as a tourist attraction and was finally sold as scrap.*

* The following sources were used for the list of ships on which my father served as captain:
1. Frederick Matthews' "American Merchant Ships," in *Marine History of the Pacific and Northwest,* edited by Gordon Newell, Superior Publishing Co., Seattle, 1966.
2. Harold Huycke, "Schooner *Snow & Burgess*—Her Conversion from Square-Rigger Rare in Marine Annals," in *Marine Digest,* S. S. Weyerhauser Co., Tacoma, Washington, Marine Digest Publishing Co., Seattle, Dec. 24, 1955.
3. John Lyman, member of the Maritime Research Society of San Diego, "Pacific Coast Sailors of World War I, 1916–1920," in *Marine Digest,* May 30–Oct. 31, 1942.
4. Edwin T. Coman, Jr. and Helen M. Gibbs, *Time, Tide and Timber—A Century of Pope and Talbot,* Stanford University Press, Stanford, California, 1949.

Glossary[*]

A.B.: Able-bodied seaman; an experienced seaman, one who is competent to steer, handle sails, and generally carry out duties on deck and in small boats.

Aft: Near or at the stern or after (i.e., rear) part of a ship.

Bark: A variant of barque. A bark is a three-, four-, or five-masted sailing vessel, square-rigged but with fore and aft sails on the mast farthest aft.

Barkentine: A sailing ship having square sails on the foremast only. There are three-, four-, and five-masted barkentines. Also known as "barquentine," but not to be confused with a "bark" or "barque," which is rigged differently.

---

[*] Some nautical terms are spoken and written in both their formal versions (i.e., as entered in dictionaries in general usage) and their informal versions (i.e., as most commonly employed on-board ship). Terms are listed here according to their formal versions (e.g., Belaying Pin), followed by comments on typical shipboard pronounciation (e.g., "b'la'ne pin").

Belay: To secure a rope around a belaying pin, or cleat.

Belaying Pin: Pronounced "b'la'ne pin" (i.e., "blane pin"). A metal pin fitted into a rack on the pinrail and to which a rope is secured.

Binnacle: The casing in which a ship's compass is housed.

Bitt: To secure a mooring rope.

Bitts: Upright wood or iron heads to which a mooring rope is secured.

Boatswain: Pronounced "bo'sun." The crew member, either seaman or officer, in charge of sails, rigging, boats, and other shipboard paraphernalia and responsible for the crew's activities in relation to these objects.

Bowsprit: A spar running out from the bow of a ship and to which the headsails are secured.

Bridge: The place from which a captain controls his ship. The bridge is an elevated position, with an unobstructed view in all directions.

Bulkhead: A vertical partition dividing a vessel into its component spaces, including cabins and watertight compartments in the hold.

Bulwarks: The wood railing or wall running along the sides of a ship above the level of the deck, as a protection against the sea and also to keep persons and objects from falling overboard.

CHART ROOM: Also known as a "chart house," the place on or near the bridge where charts, chronometer, and other navigational aids are stored and used.

CHRONOMETER: An instrument used for measuring time at sea. It is set in gimbals to compensate for the movements of the sea and is used to compute longitude and to make other navigational observations.

CLEAT: An upright device, made of metal or wood, with two arms to which a rope may be secured (i.e., "belayed").

COAMING: A low metal or wood wall erected around hatches to keep water from entering.

DAVITS: Metal structures from which lifeboats or other small boats are suspended. Davits are equipped with tackles for swinging boats out over the side of a ship and for raising and lowering them into the water.

DEEP-SIX: To throw something overboard.

DOGWATCH: The watch from 4 PM to 8 PM. It is divided into two two-hour watches, the "first dog" and the "second dog."

DONKEY ENGINE: An engine operated by steam from a small, sometimes portable boiler.

DOLPHIN (FISH): A fish *(Coryphaena hippurus),* also called "dorado." It is known for its shimmering blue-green coloring when in the water and for its change of color when taken out of the water and while dying. It has no relationship to the real dolphin *(Delphinus delphis),* a cetaceous mammal.

FLOAT: A floating dock or platform to which small boats are moored.

FORECASTLE: Commonly pronounced "fo'c's'le." The forward part of a ship, under the deck, where the crew lives.

FORECASTLE HEAD: Commonly pronounced "fo'c's'le-head." The foredeck area above the forecastle, an area used for working ropes and for observations.

GOONEY: An albatross, a large bird with a seven-foot wingspread. It is of the genus *Diomedea,* of which there are numerous species.

GUY: A rope used to steady a boom, davit, or other movable object or device. Also, to secure such a rope.

GYMBAL: Sometimes spelled "gimbal." A device by which objects can be suspended while at sea, so that the object is kept in a horizontal position while the ship pitches and rolls.

HALYARD: Rope used for raising (i.e., "hoisting") and lowering sails and flags.

HATCH: An opening in the deck to give entry into the hold of a ship.

HATCH COVER: A cover, made of wood or canvas, used to close a hatch.

HAWSER: An especially thick and sturdy rope, used for mooring a large vessel or for towing.

HOLD: A compartment for storing cargo, particularly below a ship's deck.

HOLYSTONE: A sandstone block used for scouring wet decks. The name comes from the scouring of decks for Sunday inspection.

JIB BOOM: An extension of the bowsprit, to which the jib, or foremost sail, is secured.

LAZARET: Commonly pronounced "lazareet" and sometimes spelled "lazarette." A storeroom on board ship.

LEE SIDE: The side of a ship which is away from the wind, as opposed to the "weather side," which is the side exposed to the wind.

LOG BOOK: The record book in which is recorded navigational data, log readings, weather, and other important daily information pertaining to the functioning of a ship.

LOG GLASS: Also known as "logline glass." An apparatus for measuring the rate of a ship's movement. It is used in conjunction with a logline.

LOGLINE: A plaited line of 100 or more fathoms, which is attached to the log glass. The logline is kept afloat by a "logship" or "logchip," a flat piece of wood in the shape of a quadrant and weighted at the center of the curved bottom to keep it afloat.

MAINSAIL: Often pronounced "mains'l." The large sail hoisted on the principal mast of a ship.

MATE: A ship's officer. The first mate is usually the second in command, responsible directly to the ship's captain. The number of additional mates (i.e., second mate, third mate, fourth mate, etc.) depends on the size of the ship. On larger ships, these additional mates are usually assigned special duties.

PAINTER: A rope attached to the bow of a small boat for tying it to a wharf, etc.

PIN: A vertical pin to which ropes can be secured.

PIN RAIL: A rail with holes into which pins can be inserted, so that ropes can be secured at any point along the rail.

POOP: Also called "poop deck." The aftermost deck of a ship, usually raised above the other decks and typically forming the roof of the cabin built in the stern.

PORT: The left-hand side of any vessel seen from inboard looking forward, opposite of starboard.

RED LEAD: The red oxide of lead applied to iron work to prevent rust.

SCHOONER: A sea-going vessel with fore-and-aft rigging. A schooner has two or more masts, with the larger cargo-carrying vessels typically having three or four.

SCUPPERS: Openings in the bulwarks, through which water can escape from the decks.

SKIFF: A small, light boat.

SKYSAIL: Often pronounced "skys'l." A small sail placed high on the mast.

SLOP CHEST: The chest used for storing the clothing and supplies issued to sailors during a sea voyage. Such issues were at one time called "slops."

SQUARE RIG: A vessel that has square sails set at right angles (i.e., crosswise) to the hull, as opposed to fore-and-aft sails, which are set in line with the hull.

STARBOARD: The right-hand side of a ship looking forward from inboard, opposite of port.

TAFFRAIL: A rail at the stern of a vessel.

TAR AND OAKUM: Oakum refers to old strands of rope broken down into its constituent fibers. Mixed with tar, it is used for caulking.

TELEMACHUS: In Greek legend the son of Ulysses and Penelope. In Lord Alfred Tennyson's poem *Ulysses,* the old king contemplates his life and his approaching old age and death, saying, "This is my son, mine own Telemachus, to whom I leave the sceptre and the isle. . . ." Plural: Telemachae (i.e., faithful offspring).

TONGUES AND SOUNDS: A popular dish at one time. The "tongues" of fish, along with the swimming bladders of fish, especially of ling cods and sturgeons.

TOPSAIL: Often pronounced "tops'l." Sail set above a mainsail.

TRADE WIND: Often simply referred to as "trade" or "the trades." Any wind that flows steadily in the same direction, used by seagoing sailing vessels. Also sometimes specifically applied to seasonal winds in the Indian Ocean and to winds that blow constantly toward the equator.

WATCH: A division of time, usually four hours, used for working various shipboard duties.

WEATHER SIDE: The side of a vessel on which the wind blows, as opposed to the "lee side" (i.e., protected side).

WINDJAMMER: Any large, seagoing sailing vessel.